CUTTING EDGE

THIRD EDITION

ADVANCED

TEACHER'S RESOURCE BOOK

WITH RESOURCE DISC

DAMIAN WILLIAMS

SARAH CUNNINGHAM PETER MOOR AND JONATHAN BYGRAVE

CONTENTS

TEACHER'S RESOURCE BOOK

Introduction

Teacher's notes

TEACHER'S RESOURCE DISC

Extra Resources

• Class audio scripts

• Video scripts

• Photocopiable worksheets with instructions

• Photocopiable worksheets index

Tests

• Unit tests

• Mid-course test

• End of course test

• Test audio

• Test audio script

• Downloadable test audio

• Test answer key

STUDENTS' BOOK CONTENTS

Pronunciation	Task	World culture/ Language live	Language summary and practice
Varieties of English	Give tips on learning a language well **Preparation**: Listening and reading **Task**: Speaking	**Language live** **Writing**: A report **Listening**: Varieties of English	Language summary 01, page 112 Grammar practice 01, page 114 Vocabulary practice 01, page 152
Word stress	Describe a story that provokes strong emotions **Preparation**: Listening and speaking **Task**: Speaking **Follow up**: Writing	**World culture**: Luxury superbrands	Language summary 02, page 116 Grammar practice 02, page 119 Vocabulary practice 02, page 153
	Decide which project to back **Preparation**: Reading and vocabulary **Task**: Speaking **Follow up**: Writing	**Language live** **Speaking**: Describing quantities **Writing**: Summarising statistics	Language summary 03, page 120 Grammar practice 03, page 122 Vocabulary practice 03, page 154
Accuracy	Decide who wins the award **Preparation**: Listening **Task**: Speaking **Follow up**: Writing	**World culture**: Three minutes of exercise	Language summary 04, page 124 Grammar practice 04, page 126 Vocabulary practice 04, page 155
Intonation of phrases for getting people to do something	Deal with a problem tactfully **Preparation**: Reading and vocabulary **Task**: Speaking **Follow up**: Writing	**Language live** **Writing**: Asking people to do things by email **Speaking**: Getting people to do things	Language summary 05, page 128 Grammar practice 05, page 130 Vocabulary practice 05, page 156

STUDENTS' BOOK CONTENTS

MESSAGE FROM THE AUTHORS

"Do you remember the first time you sent a text message? Or when you started checking information online? These things may seem like centuries ago or only yesterday, but one thing is for sure, in the last twenty years or so we have lived through a period of unprecedented technological change. Change which has affected all of our personal and working lives. Change that will not go away but will continue in ways that we haven't yet imagined.

Cutting Edge Advanced New Edition, while retaining its most popular features, has changed to reflect and embrace the digital age. We have done this through new texts, enhanced features and design along with a whole suite of new digital components. We've added richer and more varied video content in the *World culture* lessons which deepen learners' knowledge and understanding of global issues, direct them to purposeful, focused research on the internet and guide them to summarise their findings through guided writing tasks. *World culture* lessons also develop learners' presentation skills whilst *Language live* lessons focus on key functional areas and extend the increasingly important skill of writing.

The new Share your task feature encourages learners to film and compare their work with other *Cutting Edge* users. The fully revised *MyEnglishLab* for *Cutting Edge Advanced New Edition* has a wide variety of interactive exercises to motivate and engage learners along with the gradebook so you can keep track of your learners' progress in an instant.

Grammar rules, vocabulary lists and test scores all play their part in language learning, but that's not the whole story; in the end, language learning is about connecting people. *Cutting Edge Advanced New Edition* provides a window on the world with dramatic video clips, information-rich texts and engaging tasks. These provide a springboard for learners to engage in meaningful speaking and writing activities that reflect the reality of the 21st century.

We hope that you and your learners will enjoy using *Cutting Edge Advanced New Edition* and we would like to thank you for the invaluable input you have given us over the years. We look forward to continuing and widening our ongoing dialogue with *Cutting Edge* users all over the world."

Sarah Cunningham and Peter Moor

OVERVIEW OF COMPONENTS

STUDENTS' BOOK

- Ten units with 90 to 120 hours of teaching material
- A comprehensive Language summary with Grammar and Vocabulary Practice sections
- Audio scripts of the class audio

DVD-ROM

- Audio material for use in class
- DVD content (World culture)
- Audio and video scripts
- Digital Mini Dictionary

WORKBOOK

- Additional grammar, vocabulary and pronunciation exercises to complement the Students' Book
- Additional functional language practice exercises
- Extra listening and reading material
- Extra writing practice

WORKBOOK AUDIO

- Audio material to practice listening, pronunciation and functional language
- Visit www.english.com/students/cuttingedge3e to download the audio

MYENGLISHLAB

Learning Management System that provides:

- Interactive workbook with instant feedback
- Extra practice in grammar, vocabulary and the four skills
- Unit, Mid-course and End of course tests
- Extra videos with interactive exercises

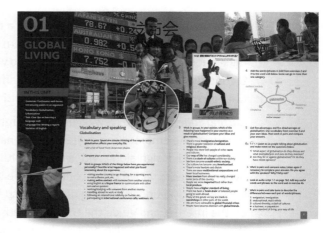

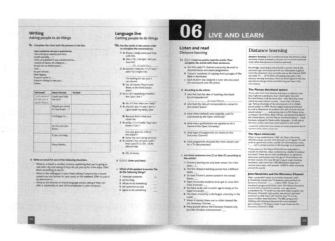

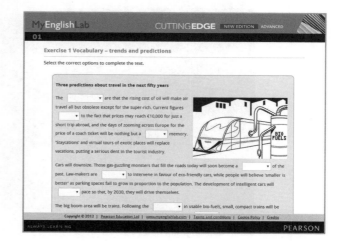

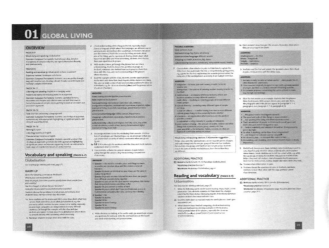

TEACHER'S RESOURCE BOOK

- Teacher's notes for every unit with alternative suggestions, culture notes and answer keys
- Generic teaching tips on useful areas such as: grammar, lexis, pronunciation, using video etc.

TEACHER'S RESOURCE DISC

- Class audio scripts and video scripts
- Photocopiable worksheets to provide additional practice of key language
- Editable and printable tests
- Test audio, audio scripts and answer keys

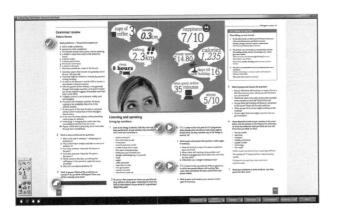

ACTIVE TEACH

Software for classroom use to help teachers get the most out of the course featuring:

- Answer reveal feature
- Integrated audio and video content
- Test master containing all course tests
- Large extra resources section
- Grammar and vocabulary review games
- A host of useful tools

WEBSITE

- Information about the course
- Sample materials
- Placement test
- A range of free downloadable worksheets

www.pearsonELT.com/cuttingedge3e

THE STUDENTS' BOOK

1 Key language highlighted at the start of each unit.

2 Topic-related vocabulary and focus on high-frequency, useful words and phrases.

3 Personalised speaking activities recycle vocabulary and encourage learners to draw on their own knowledge and experience.

4 Information-rich texts reflect learners' interests and experience.

5 A variety of pre and post-reading activities are provided to get the most out of reading texts.

6 Grammar review sections focus on major areas that learners will have some knowledge of but may need to revise e.g. continuous verb forms.

7 Plenty of form-based and communicative practice of key language.

8 Cross-referencing to *Language summary* and *Grammar Practice* sections for additional explanations and exercises.

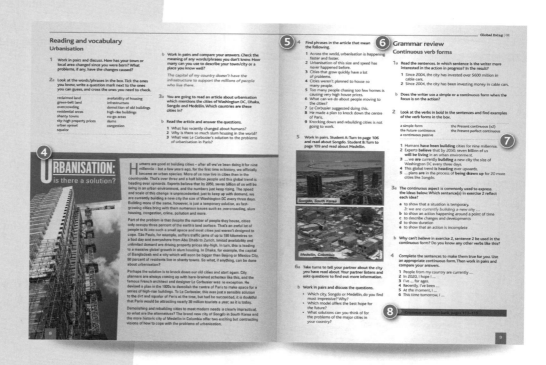

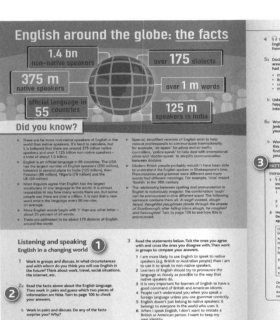

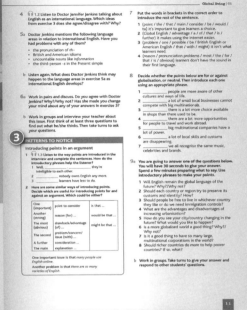

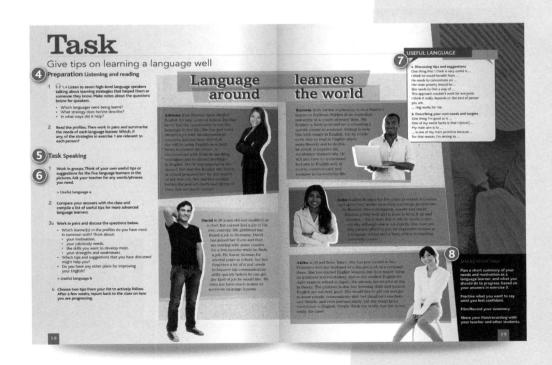

1 Listening, reading and speaking activities are integrated throughout to extend and consolidate language covered in the unit.

2 Learners are encouraged to learn more about the world and other cultures.

3 Special *Patterns to Notice* sections focus on useful phrases and patterns arising from reading and listening texts.

4 A model or stimulus is provided to show learners what they are expected to do.

5 Structured speaking tasks help learners to achieve a particular goal or outcome.

6 Learners are encouraged to think and prepare before they do the task.

7 *Useful language* boxes help learners find the right expressions.

8 *Share your task* activities encourage learners to reflect and perfect their performance.

THE STUDENTS' BOOK

1 *Language live* spreads focus on functional language and writing.

2 Writing sections focus on particular genres e.g. reports, reviews, emails etc.

3 Listening and Pronunciation sections focus on useful areas for advanced learners e.g. varieties of English.

4 *Can do* box at the end of each unit highlights what learners have achieved in the unit.

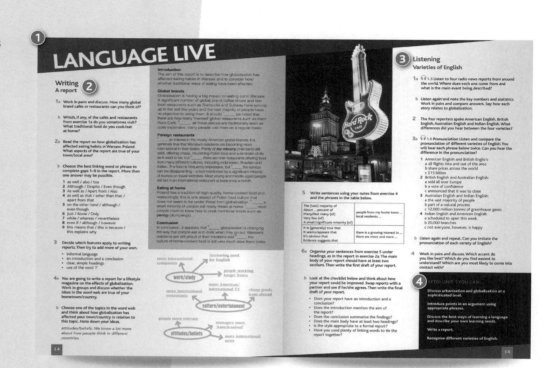

5 *World culture* spreads explore contemporary issues of global interest.

6 *Find out first/Find out more* sections develop online research and presentation skills.

7 Topics are introduced through authentic documentary-style clips from TV programmes and other sources.

8 *World view* sections encourage learners to share ideas and experiences.

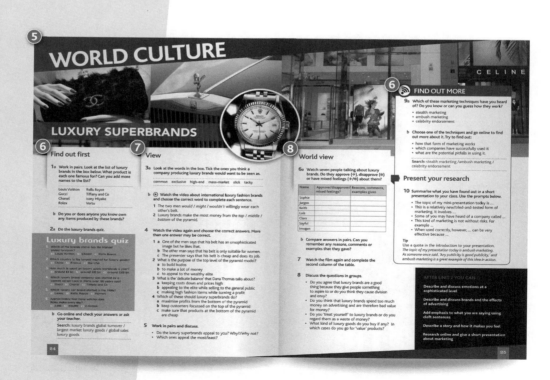

01 LANGUAGE SUMMARY

CONTINUOUS VERB FORMS

01 GRAMMAR PRACTICE

CONTINUOUS VERB FORMS

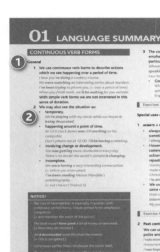

A TALL ORDER

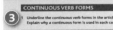

Something for everyone ☆☆☆☆

1 *Language summary* with *Grammar* and *Vocabulary Practice* sections at the back of the Students' Book ensure systematic consolidation of new language covered in the unit.

2 *Language summaries* provide comprehensive explanations and examples of language covered in the unit.

3 *Grammar Practice* sections provide exercises which can be done in class or for homework.

THE SUPPORT COMPONENTS

WORKBOOK

The Workbook contains a wide variety of grammar, vocabulary and functional language exercises that review all the areas studied in the Students' Book. It also features additional listening, reading and writing practice.

1 Writing exercises offer further practice of the genres covered in the Students' Book.

2 A variety of functional language practice activities consolidate areas covered in the Students' Book.

3 The Workbook contains regular listening practice using the accompanying audio files.

4 *Listen and read* sections encourage learners to develop listening skills using the accompanying audio files.

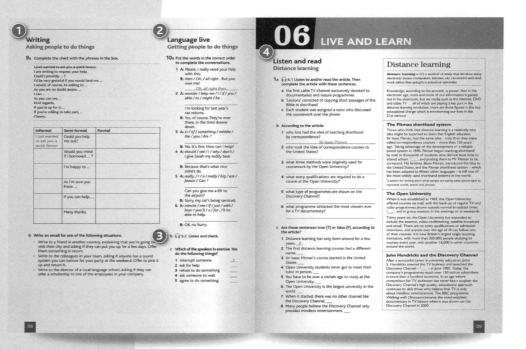

MYENGLISHLAB

MyEnglishLab provides a blended and personalised learning environment with materials that can be assigned at the touch of a button.

- Interactive Workbook exercises with instant feedback and automatic grade book.
- Common error report that highlights mistakes that learners are making.
- Tips and feedback that direct learners to reference materials and encourage them to work out answers themselves.
- Mid-course and end of course tests.
- Extra video with interactive exercises for every unit

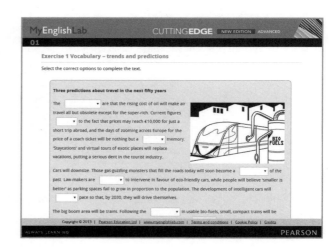

ACTIVETEACH

Cutting Edge Advanced New Edition ActiveTeach contains everything you need to make the course come alive. It includes integrated whiteboard software that allows you to add notes, embed files, save your work and reduce preparation time.

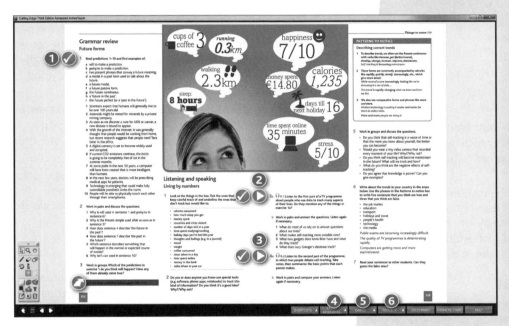

1 Answers to exercises are revealed at the touch of a button.

2 Audio and video content fully integrated with time-coded scripting.

3 Shortcuts to the relevant pages of the *Language summary* and *Grammar Practice* sections.

4 Extra resources section with photocopiables, teacher's notes, editable audio and video scripts, editable tests and more.

5 Grammar and vocabulary games for warm up and review activities.

6 Useful tools include a regular/phonetic keyboard, a stopwatch and a scorecard.

WEBSITE

The *Cutting Edge Advanced New Edition* website provides a wealth of information and additional material to support the course.
- Information about the course, its components and the authors.
- Introductory author videos.
- Sample materials and free downloadable worksheets.
- A placement test.

www.pearsonELT.com/cuttingedge3e

COURSE RATIONALE

The thinking behind Cutting Edge Advanced New Edition

Overview

Cutting Edge Advanced New Edition has a multilayered, topic-based syllabus which includes thorough and comprehensive work on grammar, vocabulary, pronunciation and the skills of listening, reading, speaking and writing. Structured speaking tasks form a central part of each unit.

Cutting Edge Advanced New Edition gives special emphasis to:

- communication
- the use of phrases and collocations
- active learning and research skills.
- recycling and revision.

Topics and content

We aim to motivate learners with units based around up-to-date, globally relevant topics which help them gather information about the world and other cultures through the medium of English.

Cutting Edge Advanced New Edition provides learners with many opportunities to share their opinions about the topics in focus and personalisation is strongly emphasized throughout. The differing needs of monocultural and multicultural classes has also been kept in mind throughout.

Approach to grammar

Learners are encouraged to take an active, systematic approach to developing their knowledge of grammar, and to use new language in a natural, communicative way.

Typically, there is at least one major *Grammar review* section in each unit, in which a broad area of grammar is presented that learners will probably already have considerable knowledge of, for e.g. Perfect verb forms, Modals, time and tense etc. The material in the *Grammar reviews* is designed to allow teachers and students to find out which rules about the given language area are already familiar and which require further clarification and practice, as well as provide some communicative practice of the area as a whole. Each *Grammar review* is related to the topic of the unit, but is designed to 'stand alone': this means that it can be omitted completely if your students do not need work on the area in question, or can be covered at a different point in the unit if this works more logically for the class.

In addition to the *Grammar reviews*, each unit of the *Cutting Edge Advanced Students' Book* also has a *Patterns to notice* section. Featuring examples of language taken from the preceding listening or reading texts, these sections are designed to focus learners' attention on a variety of useful phrases and patterns, e.g. describing typical habits, adding emphasis with auxiliaries and inversion.

The *Grammar review* and *Patterns to notice* sections in *Cutting Edge Advanced New Edition* are followed up thoroughly through:

- a wide range of communicative and written practice exercises in the Students' Book
- the opportunity to use new grammar naturally in the speaking tasks (see below)
- the *Language summary* and *Grammar Practice* sections which consolidate learning and clarify problems
- further written practice in the *Workbook* and interactive exercises in the fully revised *MyEnglishLab*.

(See *Teaching tips: Working with grammar* on page 20, and *Using the Grammar extension bank* on page 25.)

Approach to vocabulary

A wide vocabulary is vital to communicative success, so new lexis is introduced and practised at every stage in the course. Particular attention has been paid to the selection of high-frequency, internationally useful words and phrases, using information from the British National Corpus.

Vocabulary input is closely related to the topics and tasks in the units, allowing for plenty of natural recycling. Further practice is provided in the *Vocabulary practice* sections at the back of the book and in the *Workbook*.

Fluent speakers make extensive use of 'prefabricated chunks' of language. *Cutting Edge Advanced New Edition* gives particular emphasis to collocations and fixed phrases which are integrated throughout in:

- topic-based vocabulary lessons
- the *Useful language* boxes in the speaking tasks
- *Language live* lessons, which focus on phrases used in complex functional areas such as expressing quantities, getting people to do things, explaining technical problems etc.

(See *Teaching tips: Working with lexis* on page 21.)

The speaking tasks

Cutting Edge Advanced New Edition integrates elements of a task-based approach into its methodology. Each unit has a structured speaking task including surveys, mini-talks, problem-solving and narrative tasks. The primary focus is on achieving a particular outcome or product, rather than on practising specific language. The tasks provide the opportunity for realistic and extended communication, and because learners are striving to express what they want to say, they are more likely to absorb the language that they are learning. The tasks are graded carefully in terms of difficulty and, in order for them to work effectively, a model or stimulus is provided, useful language is given to help learners express themselves and thinking/planning time is included. Learners are also encouraged to record themselves or each other performing the tasks, and to share their recording with other learners through the new *Share your task* feature, thus providing extra motivation for rehearsal and accurate production.

(See *Teaching tips: Making tasks work* on page 23, and *Teaching advanced learners* on page 26.)

World culture

The *World culture* pages are a new feature of *Cutting Edge Advanced New Edition* and are designed to deepen learners' knowledge and understanding of global issues. This is done through the use of authentic video clips which act as a stimulus for internet-based research around the issues raised in the video. Learners are guided through the necessary steps to make their research focused and productive, and are given guidance on how to summarise their research through a guided written and/or spoken follow-up in the form of a presentation. The emphasis throughout is on creating a link between the classroom and the outside world, and the development of research skills which will prove of lasting value.

Language live

The *Language live* pages are another new feature of *Cutting Edge Advanced New Edition*. The main purpose of these pages is to help learners to deal with more complex functional areas such as expressing quantities, asking people to do things, explaining technical problems etc. The *Language live* pages also develop the important skill of writing with a focus on useful genres such as writing reports, reviews, letters and emails.

Other features of *Cutting Edge Advanced New Edition*

Listening

Cutting Edge Advanced New Edition places strong emphasis on listening. Listening material consists of:

• short extracts and mini-dialogues to introduce and practise new language

• words and sentences for close listening and to model pronunciation

• longer texts (interviews, stories and conversations) which often feature in the Preparation section as a model or stimulus for the Task

• regular *Listen and read* sections in the *Workbook* to further develop learners' confidence in this area.

Speaking

There is also a strong emphasis on speaking, as follows:

• The tasks provide a regular opportunity for extended and prepared speaking based around realistic topics and situations.

• Much of the practice of grammar and lexis is through oral exercises and activities.

• The topics and reading texts in each unit provide opportunities for follow-up discussion.

• There is regular integrated work on pronunciation.

• Most of the photocopiable activities in the *Teacher's Resource Disc* involve extensive speaking practice.

Reading

The course features a wide range of reading material including newspaper and website articles, factual/scientific texts, stories, letters, blogs and emails. The texts are primarily designed to develop reading skills and many lead into grammar work and language analysis. Some texts also provide a model or stimulus for tasks and models for writing activities.

Writing

Regular and systematic work on writing skills are developed in *Cutting Edge Advanced New Edition* through:

• *Language live* pages in the *Students' Book*, which focus on writing e-mails and letters, writing narratives and reviews etc.

• *Writing* sections in the *Workbook*, which expand on the areas covered in the *Students' Book*

• written follow-up sections to many of the speaking tasks.

Pronunciation

Pronunciation work in *Cutting Edge Advanced New Edition* is integrated with grammar and lexis and there are special pronunciation sections in every unit. The focus is mainly on stress, weak forms and intonation. A range of activity types are used, including discrimination exercises and dictation, and an equal emphasis is placed on understanding and reproducing.

Learning skills

Cutting Edge Advanced New Edition develops learning skills in a number of ways:

• The approach to grammar encourages learners to experiment with language and to work out rules for themselves.

• The task-based approach encourages learners to take a pro-active role in their learning.

• Many activities in the Students' books focus on useful learning strategies, and learners are encouraged throughout to share ideas about the most effective ways to learn.

Revision and recycling

Recycling is a key feature of *Cutting Edge Advanced New Edition*. New language is explicitly recycled through:

• speaking tasks which offer constant opportunities for learners to use what they have studied in a natural way, and for teachers to assess their progress and remind them of important points.

• extra practice exercises in the *Grammar and Vocabulary practice* sections. These are designed to cover all the main grammar and vocabulary areas in the unit. After trying the exercises, learners are encouraged to return to any parts of the unit that they still feel unsure about to assess what they have (and have not) remembered.

(See *Teaching tips: Making tasks work* on page 23 and *Using Grammar extension bank and Vocabulary practice* sections on page 25.)

TEACHING TIPS

*How to get the most out of Cutting Edge
Advanced New Edition*

Using a discovery approach to grammar

Cutting Edge Advanced New Edition often uses a 'discovery' approach to grammar because we believe that learners absorb rules best if they work them out for themselves. Learners at this level often have some previous knowledge of the language but this is often difficult for the teacher to predict. The 'test-teach' exercises in the *Grammar review* sections are designed so that learners can utilise this knowledge, and so that teachers can adjust their approach to take account of it.

1 Get to know the material available

Each unit of *Cutting Edge Advanced New Edition Students' Book* contains:

• a *Grammar review* section reviewing and bringing together a major area of grammar that learners will already have considerable knowledge of, e.g. Perfect verb forms, Modals.

• a *Grammar extension bank* at the back of the book. This contains a *Language summary* section providing more detailed information about what is covered in the *Grammar review* sections, and a *Grammar practice* section providing a range of written and oral practice exercises. These practise more complex or challenging points from the *Language summary*, and revise areas which should be familiar.

• a *Patterns to notice* section focusing students on and providing practice of a variety of useful phrases and patterns, e.g. Describing typical habits, Patterns with comparatives and superlatives, Adding emphasis with auxiliaries and inversion.

In addition to this, the *Cutting Edge Advanced New Edition Workbook* includes consolidation exercises for all the points in the *Language summary* as well as further practice of the *Patterns to notice* sections.

The *Cutting Edge Advanced New Edition Teacher's Resource Disc* also includes two photocopiable grammar activities for each unit.

2 Use a diagnostic approach

The *Grammar review* sections are designed to allow the teacher and students to find out which rules about the given language area are already familiar and which require further clarification and practice, as well as provide some communicative practice of the area as a whole. In the exercises in this section, learners are usually required to identify and/or classify different examples of the language, and are then guided by a series of questions to work out rules and form hypotheses about the area, which should help them to gain a more global understanding of it. As different learners are likely to know different things, they can be encouraged to share what they know by working on these exercises in pairs or groups. When you go through the answers to the exercises, it is often useful to elicit or give one or two further examples of the rule: suggestions for these are included in the teacher's

notes for each unit. When gaps in students' knowledge are revealed, you can refer them to the relevant section of the *Language summary*, which also contains cross references to appropriate exercises in the *Grammar practice* section. You may want to read through the section(s) of the *Language summary* with the learners, and give them the practice exercise(s) to do in class time, or it may be more appropriate to direct students to do this reading and practice for homework.

3 Focus on learners' needs and interests

Each *Grammar review* section is related to the topic of the unit, but is designed to 'stand alone': this means that it can be omitted completely, or can be covered at a different point in the unit if this works more logically for your particular class.

If the majority of your learners do not want to spend class time on grammar because they feel, for example, that speaking and listening are their priorities, the *Grammar review* section can be set for homework. Learners work through the exercises and study the relevant sections of the *Language summary* at home, then come to class with any outstanding queries – these can be dealt with at the beginning or end of the next lesson, or on an individual basis, e.g. during tutorial time.

4 Pull things together

It is likely that learners have mostly studied grammar in a 'linear' fashion up to now, learning individual structures one after the other, and revisiting them several times. At this level they will have come across almost all English grammar at one stage or another. This is an opportunity, therefore, to pull it all together, by looking at common features of large areas of grammar. For example, in Unit 2, the way the perfect aspect links together two time periods is highlighted. By pulling things together in this way, learners gain insight into the way the grammar of the language works as a whole.

5 Use the Patterns to notice sections

The examples for the *Patterns to notice* sections are always taken from the listening or reading material that immediately precedes it in the unit, e.g. in Unit 8, patterns for 'describing typical habits' are taken from the preceding listening section. These and further examples are given in a box, and learners are asked to 'notice' how they are formed and used. This is followed by an exercise for practice. If you want to help learners to 'process' these patterns more actively before they look at the examples and explanation in the box, you could:

• split the phrases in half and write them on slips of paper for learners to match up, working in small groups, each with a set of slips.

• write the phrases on the board with gaps in them, for learners to discuss and try to complete.

• write the phrases on the board with the words in the wrong order, for learners to discuss and put into the correct order.

Before going on to the practice exercise, you may also want to help learners to pronounce the patterns naturally, by asking them where the main stress falls, highlighting any features of connected speech and having them repeat some of the examples.

Working with lexis

1 Focus on phrases and collocations

Advanced learners often mistakenly assume that in order to make their vocabulary sound more advanced, they need to know a lot of complex, long words: the danger of this is that their speech and writing will start to sound very unnatural. Point out to learners that it is often a question of adding more varied word combinations to their existing knowledge, for example 'tell' not only collocates with 'a lie', 'the truth', 'a story', etc. but can also be used with the following, more unusual words and phrases:

2 Encourage learners to notice patterns

In today's online world it's likely that learners come across English all the time, by using social media, watching films, etc. Encourage learners to be aware of the language they see and hear, by highlighting key phrases and patterns when working with text in class. This will hopefully encourage learners to continue doing so outside the classroom.

3 Feed in phrases on a 'little but often' basis

To avoid overloading learners and ensure that your lexical input is useful, teach a few phrases relating to particular activities as you go along. For example, in a grammar practice activity, instead of simple answers such as *Yes, I do* or *No, I haven't*, feed in phrases such as *It depends, I don't really care, I would probably* ... . The same is true of discussions about reading / listening texts and writing activities.

4 Focus on guessing meaning from context

Advanced learners need to practise guessing the meaning of unfamiliar words and phrases during class time, so that they become more efficient and independent readers outside the classroom. It will also be important for learners preparing for examinations where there is a large amount of reading material and dictionary use is not permitted. Many of the reading texts in *Cutting Edge Advanced New Edition* have an accompanying exercise where students are required to guess the meaning of certain words/phrases, sometimes with the help of definitions to match. This vocabulary is not very high frequency, and is not intended to be activated: it is more important that students learn to use the surrounding text to help them determine its meaning. You could show students how to do this by doing an example with a 'nonsense' word, for example:

'We put the *grubble* back in its box and closed the lid carefully, so that it couldn't escape.'

We know that:

- 'grubble' is a noun, because it has 'the' in front of it.
- a 'grubble' is alive, because it could escape – it must be a type of animal, insect or bird.
- a 'grubble' is small enough to be put into a box.

5 Encourage learners to keep a vocabulary book

Students need to record and organise new words and phrases in a way that will make them easily accessible and memorable. You might like to suggest that they keep a separate vocabulary book for this purpose. You could also remind them of useful habits to get into when they are recording new words and phrases. The following techniques will help students to record and memorise new vocabulary more effectively:

- writing the word or phrase in an example sentence.
- highlighting collocations.
- marking the stress on words of more than one syllable.
- including an explanation or translation of the meaning, if necessary.
- using an illustration if they find this helpful.

Each page of the vocabulary book or file can be organised around a topic (for example 'money') or a key word (for example 'tell'). Students can then add to the page when they come across new words or phrases related to that topic or key word.

6 Reinforce and recycle phrases

This is particularly important with phrases which, for the reasons given above, can be hard to remember. Most revision games and activities teachers do with single items of vocabulary can be adapted and used with phrases. You may find the following useful in addition:

- **Make a phrase bank:**
  Copy new words and phrases from the lesson onto slips of card or paper (large enough for learners to read if you hold them up at the front of the room) and keep them in a box or bag, or save them in a file if you are using an interactive whiteboard. This is a good record for you, as well as your learners, of the phrases that the class has studied – do this frequently at the start and end of lessons to recycle the phrases often. Hold them up or display them, and ask learners to give you (choose as appropriate):
  – an explanation or translation of the phrase
  – synonyms
  – opposites
  – the pronunciation
  – situations where they might say this
  – a sentence including the phrase
  – the missing word that you are holding your hand over (for example, *on* in the phrase *get on well with*)
  – the phrase itself, based on a definition or translation that you have given them.

- **Have learners create their own review materials:**
  Take several small strips of paper into class, enough for a few for each learner. Ask them to look back over their notes (or in the *Vocabulary practice* sections at the back of the book) and choose 3–4 phrases they've learnt recently and write each one on a strip of paper. Circulate and check learners have formed the phrases correctly. Learners then tear each strip into separate words, shuffle them all together and give them to a partner, to put in order.

TEACHING TIPS

How to get the most out of Cutting Edge Advanced New Edition

Helping students with pronunciation

1 Aim for intelligibility

Advanced learners worry just as much as others about their pronunciation, and appreciate taking time to work on speaking clearly. However, in today's world there are more speakers of English as a foreign or second language than there are native speakers, and so no-one can really say they 'own' the language or speak the most 'correct' form. Having an accent when using English also helps learners retain their identity. It is therefore best to encourage learners to make themselves understood rather than aim for 'perfect' pronunciation, whatever that might be.

Consonants (particularly at the beginning and end of words) are probably more important than vowels here. Use any tips you know for helping learners to reproduce them. You might focus them on a similar sound in their own language and then help them to adapt it, or use a trick like starting with /u.../ to get learners to produce the /w/ sound. Anything that works is valid here! Sometimes it is useful to contrast the problem sound with the one that learners are mistakenly producing, via a 'minimal pair' such as *best* and *vest*. Say the pair of words several times, and then ask learners to say which they can hear, before asking them to produce the words themselves.

2 Little and often is a good principle

There are regular *Pronunciation* boxes in the *Students' Book* but you should aim to integrate pronunciation work whenever learners have a problem. 'Little and often' also applies here. On the other hand, think about what you want to achieve: clarity and confidence are what most learners need, rather than perfection in every detail. Individuals vary widely in what they can achieve, so don't push too much when a particular student is getting frustrated or embarrassed.

3 Drill in different ways

Choral and/or individual repetition is the simplest and most effective pronunciation activity. It can help to build confidence by giving learners valuable practice in a 'safe' environment. There are different ways to drill language, and it's important to vary the way we do it. Here are some tips to remember:

- **When drilling longer phrases:**
  Establish a rhythm and start by drilling only the stressed syllables. For example, for the phrase *What do you usually do at the weekend?* Start with *What – us – do – week*. Keeping the same rhythm, 'cram' in the other syllables, pronouncing them naturally. This helps learners feel how we use weak forms and sentence stress in English.

- **Drill the phrase backward to keep it sounding natural:**
  With longer words and phrases, start from the end and drill backwards. For example, with the word *comfortable*, work backwards *-ble – table – comfortable*. This allows you to isolate difficult parts of the word or phrase, but keep a natural-sounding pronunciation.

- **Vary your voice:**
  This can be a simple way to add variety to drills, by e.g. shouting or whispering. It also gives learners different ways to practise saying the language.

4 Focus consistently on stress

Get into the habit of focusing on word and sentence stress whenever you teach a new word/phrase with potential problems. If learners have problems, try one of the following ideas when you drill:

- Exaggerate the stress.
- Clap or click your fingers on the stressed syllable.
- Mumble the stress pattern, before saying the word: *mm-MM-mm* attention.
- Isolate the stressed syllable first, and then add the other syllables.

Don't forget to mark stressed syllables when you write new words on the board, and encourage learners to do the same when they write in their notebooks.

5 Focus on weak forms and word linking

As learners become more advanced, these features will also contribute to comprehensibility and fluency, and at any level they are important for the purposes of listening. As you teach new phrases and structures, draw learners' attention to weak forms and word linking as appropriate, and give them the opportunity to practise them, such as by using rhythm when drilling. However, do not worry too much if they do not produce the weak forms and word linking spontaneously – this is likely to come naturally when learners become more fluent.

6 Make learners aware of intonation

There are few situations in which wrong intonation leads to serious misunderstanding. Where problems do occasionally occur is in the area of politeness, and sounding sufficiently enthusiastic or over-entusiastic. In *Cutting Edge Advanced New Edition*, we focus on these limited areas for intonation work. You shouldn't expect your learners to produce perfect intonation, but instead aim to raise awareness of it when appropriate. If learners have problems hearing and reproducing the intonation patterns, try some of the following ideas:

- Exaggerate the intonation pattern, before returning to a more normal model.
- Hum the intonation pattern before repeating the words.
- Use gestures to show the intonation pattern.
- Mark the intonation on the board using arrows.

If learners are getting frustrated, or cannot 'get' the correct intonation, it is probably best to come back to it another time.

Making tasks work

1 Use the task as an end in itself

The main objective of the extended speaking tasks in *Cutting Edge Advanced New Edition* is for students to use the language that they know in order to achieve a communicative goal. Each task can be seen as an opportunity for students to gain confidence in speaking and improve their speaking skills, but should not be seen as an opportunity for students to 'practise' specific language. The important thing to remember is to treat the speaking task as an end in itself rather than as a vehicle for practising new language.

2 Remember to 'personalise' the task

As a general rule, the Tasks in *Cutting Edge Advanced New Edition* have a model or stimulus to introduce them. Sometimes these are recordings of people talking about something personal, such as practical language learning tips (See *Unit 1: Give tips on learning a language well*), something they love or hate (See *Unit 8: Rant or rave*), or true/false facts about their life (See *Unit 10: Detect the lies*).

However, students are often more motivated by finding out about **you**, their teacher, so these are good opportunities for you to provide a personalised model instead. In some cases a model is not appropriate because it would pre-empt the task itself (e.g. *Unit 8: Choose celebrities for a charity trek*). In cases like this, you could consider providing a model after the task, for students to compare the outcome with their own. You could then spend some time analysing the language used (See point 5: *Provide further input and correction after the task*).

3 Use the *Useful language* boxes in different ways

Each task is accompanied by a *Useful language* box containing phrases which can be adapted by individual learners to express different ideas and opinions. These are not intended to be prescriptive, but to provide learners with a range of tools to achieve the task itself. They also provide an opportunity to listen to the phrases used by speakers doing a similar task, and in some units there is a specific exercise where students listen and tick the phrases they hear. You can vary the way you do this by:

- Giving learners a minute or two to say the phrases quietly to themselves so they know what to listen for.
- Getting learners to listen for phrases under different sections of the *Useful language* box and then sharing answers.
- Getting learners to think of possible endings for the phrases and then reading them out for their partner to guess.

4 Give students time to think and plan

Planning time is a vital opportunity for students to focus on accuracy. It is also important for building the confidence of students who are normally reluctant to speak in class. The time needed will vary from task to task, from about five to twenty minutes. This planning time may take a little getting used to at first, and, it is important to explain the rationale for planning time, and to make it clear that you will be available throughout to answer students' queries.

5 Provide further input and correction after the task

Students are more likely to retain language for which they have a genuine need. It is therefore important to provide feedback on the language that students used, or could have used, during the task. Points for this feedback stage can be noted down:

- during the planning stage, e.g. if students ask you for words or phrases which would be useful for the whole class.
- during the performance of the task, e.g. if you hear errors, or examples of language which is accurate but not natural.
- during the replaying of an audio or video recording of students performing the task.

It is important to maintain student interest throughout this feedback stage, so it should not be too long, and should contain language input which is useful and at an appropriate level for most students in the class.

6 Use the *Share your task* box

All the tasks in *Cutting Edge Advanced New Edition* have a *Share your task* box which can either be done completely in class or as a combination of homework and classwork. These offer learners the opportunity to repeat or carry out a similar task and film or record it, enabling them to consolidate what they have learnt, and put into practice any suggestions and corrections that you have discussed. This is also an opportunity for learners to practise 'perfecting' what they say when reporting on the task, in order to record a version of themselves using English to a high standard, which should be motivating. Some ideas for filming/recording include:

- learners create a video of themselves doing the task.
- learners create a TV/radio programme with a 'presenter' who introduces different people doing the task.
- learners could act out part of a narrative as a short film.
- encourage learners to add music or other background noise/visuals, and to film in different locations.
- encourage learners to post their recording on a blog or social networking site and collect comments to share with the class.
- learners watch/listen to other learners' recordings, or show them to another class, and choose the best one.
- after learners have filmed/recorded themselves, collect in the recordings and plan a 'find someone who' task. Give learners a list of things which appear in their classmates' tasks and ask them to discuss whose task each thing appears in. They then watch/listen and check their answers.
- learners watch/listen to their classmates' tasks and then write a summary report.

See the Teacher's notes for further suggestions on how to use each *Share your task* box.

TEACHING TIPS

How to get the most out of Cutting Edge Advanced New Edition

Using video material in class

The video lessons are a new feature of *Cutting Edge Advanced New Edition*, and are intended to be modern, engaging ways of consolidating and extending some of the topics covered in the units. The video lessons occur at the end of every other unit and are called *World culture*.

World culture lessons:

These contain two clips per unit: part of a TV programme and *World view* clips, which include short 'talking heads' style interviews, where people give their opinions on the topics covered in the programme. They are intended to encourage learners to explore contemporary topics and develop the important 21st century skill of online research.

1 Using video in class

Video can be an excellent way to study language as it is not only motivating but also illustrates the importance of non-verbal aspects of communication. In many respects, it is the 'next best thing' to observing real life. In order to get the best out of it though, observe the following guidelines:

- **Watch the clip yourself beforehand:**
  It is important to know what to expect so you can help learners to understand the clip.

- **Do something visual first:**
  The exercises in *Cutting Edge Advanced New Edition* are designed to go from easier to more challenging, but sometimes, especially at this level, you might find that they'll benefit from first just watching the clip to get a general idea of what it's about, before watching again and doing the exercises in the *Students' Book*.

  You could also show the clip with the sound off, and ask learners to guess what it's about in pairs, before playing again with the sound on for them to check their ideas.

- **Do not replay the clip too many times:**
  Learners may become demotivated if they really can't understand something in it. Instead, make the most of the subtitles or time-coded scripts (see above). Always give learners a chance to comprehend by viewing only first, but if they run into difficulties with a particular part of the clip, use the subtitles/scripts to pinpoint the difficult language and explain as necessary.

- **Vary how you use it:**
  There are many different ways of using video in class, with different purposes. For example, learners can sit in pairs, one facing the screen and the other with their back to it. Play the clip with the sound off, and the learner facing the screen describes what happens to the other learner, who then watches afterwards and checks. You'll find more suggestions in the teacher's notes for each lesson, and it's a good idea to vary the way you use the video material in class to keep it interesting.

2 Doing online research

The *World culture* lessons involve two opportunities for learners to do online research. Firstly, in the Find out first section where they collect background information on the topic of the video, and secondly after the *World view* section when they find out about further things related to the topic of the video. This is an important 21st century skill for learners to master in English, and so the following ideas may help:

- **Make the most of available technology:**
  If learners have smartphones, they can use them to do the research. If not, you can set it for homework: before the class for the *Find out first* sections and after class for the research later in the lesson.

- **Vary the way in which learners do research:**
  In one lesson learners can research alone then compare answers in pairs, and in the next lesson they could research in pairs, then pool ideas as a class or in groups. Vary the way in which learners research, too, so rather than just using the same search engine, different learners could enter the search terms into different encyclopedia sites, forums, etc., and compare results.

- **Be on hand to help:**
  Since there are very few limits as to what's available online, circulate and be available to help with language, and also to step in in the case of inappropriate search results.

- **Encourage learners to prioritise information:**
  Part of being a good researcher is not just obtaining results but also prioritising the most important points. Encourage learners to do this by asking them to find no more than three facts, for example, or only noting down facts which they can find on more than one website.

- **Encourage learners to be critical thinkers:**
  There is a lot of information available on the internet, and not all of it is always reliable! Encourage learners to question information they find, and corroborate it with other learners. How reputable is the website where they found the information? Whether they can prove what they've found clearly is perhaps not as important as encouraging them to question everything.

Using the Grammar extension bank

This contains two parts for each unit of the *Students' book*:

- a *Language summary* section providing more detailed and comprehensive information about what is covered in the *Grammar review* sections
- a *Grammar practice* section providing a range of written and oral practice exercises. These exercises practise more complex or challenging points from the *Language summary*, as well as revise areas which should be familiar at this level.

The exercises in the *Grammar extension bank* are designed for students to do in pairs or alone. If it is clear that a certain language point is new and/or causing confusion for the majority of students, you can set the relevant practice exercise for them to work on in class time, and go through the answers together. However, students are likely to have different needs, e.g. if some are preparing for an exam and others are not. Answers are provided in the *Teacher's book* for teachers to photocopy. There are various different ways in which you can use this section:

1 Use the Grammar extension bank sections to consolidate learning

The *Language summary* sections provide a comprehensive overview of each language point covered in the main unit. These can be used in different ways. For example:

- learners read the *Language summary* section before focusing on the *Grammar review* section in the main unit.
- after clarifying the language in the lesson, give learners a few minutes to read the relevant section(s) of the *Language summary* to consolidate what they have learnt, and think of questions to ask you.
- learners read the *Language summary* for homework, either before or after the class, and think of questions they would like to ask.

2 Use the Grammar practice sections for further practice

If you think your learners need additional practice before attempting the more communicative activities in the main units, you could select one or two of the *Grammar practice* activities to do in class first. Learners do the relevant exercises alone or in pairs after reviewing the language, then go back to the main unit to do the more communicative activities.

3 Use the different activities as warmers and fillers

The activities in the *Grammar practice* sections can be used when you have ten or fifteen minutes to spare. For example, you could ask students to read the *Language summary* at the end of one lesson, and do the exercises in the *Grammar practice* in another lesson.

4 Set homework based on these sections

If you are short of time in class, the *Grammar practice* section could easily be set as homework. If you do this, it might be useful to explain in class where learners should look in the *Language summary* if they need to do further revision.

5 Set aside time for learners' questions

If you set the *Grammar practice* sections for homework, in the next lesson set aside some time for learners to ask any questions they have. You could encourage learners to discuss their questions in small groups before answering them with the whole class. This is likely to be more productive if you let learners know beforehand that this time will be available and ask them to note any questions they have while they do the activities.

6 Encourage learners to take responsibility for their own progress

The approach in the *Grammar extension bank* is to encourage learner independence and personal responsibility for progress. By using these sections frequently and in different ways, you will provide opportunities for learners to reflect on their learning.

Using the vocabulary practice section

Each unit of the *Vocabulary practice* section is linked to the same unit of the *Students' Book* and contains:

- two exercises for further practice of the main vocabulary of the unit.
- a list of other words, collocations and phrases from each unit, with definitions and example sentences, followed by a practice exercise.

1 Use it as a testing device

The exercises can be done after completing the main unit. You could use it as a short test, after completing the unit in the *Students' book*. Students could prepare by reading through the definitions at home, then do the gap fill exercises as a test when they come to class. Alternatively, get students to 'test' each other on the *other words and phrases* – one reads out a definition and their partner tries to guess the phrase.

2 Use it as further practice

You could also use the exercises while working through the unit, to give further practice of the vocabulary before going back and doing the more communicative exercises in the main unit.

3 Use it as a self-study section

Learners can choose which areas they need further practice in, and do the relevant exercises for homework. Answers are provided in the *Teacher's book* for teachers to photocopy and give out the next class.

4 Make the most of the *Other words and phrases* sections

These sections aim to give additional information about words and phrases which appear less often in each unit. Encourage students to read and add to these sections.

You can also use these lists towards the end of each unit to plan recycling activities (see *Teaching tips: Working with lexis above*)

TEACHING TIPS

How to get the most out of Cutting Edge Advanced New Edition

Teaching advanced learners

1 Dealing with diverse needs

Many teachers find that students at advanced level have more diverse needs (or are more able to identify and vocalise them) than students at lower levels, e.g. some students may be preparing for an examination, while others need to write letters and emails in English at work, or want to improve listening skills so they can understand lectures or films. You can deal with this by:

• making the most of opportunities for individualisation, e.g. providing individual students with language they need during the *task preparation* stages, helping students to choose exercises from the *Grammar extension bank*, providing feedback on written work, so students can take this into account when writing the next draft.

• providing regular tutorials: while the class works on writing or grammar practice exercises, spend about ten minutes with individuals, discussing their progress and giving them suggestions for how to improve in key areas. Students appreciate the individual attention and can take the opportunity to ask you questions.

• involving students in discussion about what kind of activities they would like to spend more/less class time on.

2 Encourage students to take responsibility

For many students, this is the 'key' to progress. You can help advanced learners progress by encouraging them to:

• read in English as much as possible outside class: to expand their vocabulary, students could choose an article and underline collocations and useful phrases. They could also bring any articles of particular interest to class for discussion.

• change the language of their mobile phone to English in order to get regular practice.

• follow up an area of interest after a lesson by doing some research: this could mean researching a challenging grammar point, or using the Internet to find out more about a topic.

3 Provide students with enough challenge

Advanced learners often lose interest if they do not find their lessons challenging. It is therefore important to be flexible in your approach to the material in the course: be prepared to spend less time on a particular section, or omit it completely, if you feel it will not challenge students sufficiently.

It is also common to find advanced students who understand and can talk about quite complex grammar points, but still avoid using them in their speaking and writing. You can challenge students to use more complex language by:

• recording or making notes on part of a discussion or role play and pointing out to students how they could improve.

• giving students time to prepare what they are going to say (this is a feature of all the *Tasks* in *Cutting Edge*).

• highlighting sections of written work where you feel students could have used more ambitious language.

4 Balance accuracy and fluency

Fluency is usually perceived as the goal of most advanced learners, and teachers are often wary of correcting too much or of drilling new vocabulary or grammar. However, advanced students also perceive a need for correction and accuracy work – it is really a question of how much to do and when to do it. You could discuss this with the class before a speaking activity, and find out how much correction individuals want. It is important to distinguish between 'on the spot' correction, which can interrupt a student's 'flow' and should be used sparingly, and 'post fluency correction' which is done after the speaking activity and can provide students with a lot of valuable feedback. Students at this level will also benefit from drilling, as long as it is not 'overdone': drilling phrases and *Patterns to notice*, will not only help students with pronunciation, but will also help them to remember and retrieve language more quickly and easily.

5 Experiment with new ideas

Advanced learners have usually been learning for quite a long time, and as such will have tried lots of different ways of learning. Use this as an opportunity to try new ideas, such as discussing topics in the news. Advanced learners have more language at their disposal, and so may be better able to handle more sensitive topics.

At this level, learners may have a clear idea of how they need to use English outside the classroom, such as giving presentations, telephoning, etc. Try to find out what their needs are and practise these in class, giving feedback and suggestions. It is also a good idea to make the most of the Alternative suggestions in the teacher's notes. These often provide additional or alternative ideas for activities. When you try something new, involve the learners by explaining the aims of what you're doing and why you're doing it. Ask for their feedback afterwards.

6 Do not stop correcting errors

Learners at this level have a lot of language at their disposal, and in their quest for learning more challenging aspects of English, may pay less attention to the more basic aspects, especially when tired or not fully concentrating. Research shows that use of the third person -s, for example, is one of the last features of English to be truly acquired. This is why it is common to hear higher level learners make mistakes such as *She don't like it*. Most of the time these are 'slips' rather than errors due to lack of knowledge, and can be dealt with quickly and efficiently with simple prompting for learners to correct themselves.

Do plenty of error correction, making use of a range of techniques to pick up on these 'slips' frequently as they occur, and without drawing too much attention to them so as not to distract learners 'in the flow' too much. Little and often is the key, and building error correction techniques into your regular teaching will be much appreciated by your learners.

TEACHER'S NOTES INDEX

01 GLOBAL LIVING

OVERVIEW

PAGES 6–7

Vocabulary and speaking: Globalisation

Common European Framework: Students give clear, detailed descriptions of complex subjects; can express themselves fluently and spontaneously.

PAGES 8–9

Reading and vocabulary: Urbanisation: Is there a solution?

Grammar review: Continuous verb forms

Common European Framework: Students can scan quickly through long and complex texts, locating relevant details; can understand and exchange complex information.

PAGES 10–11

Listening and speaking: English in a changing world

Patterns to notice: Introducing points in an argument

Common European Framework: Students can follow lectures, discussions and debates with relative ease; can hold their own in formal discussion of complex issues, putting forward an articulate and persuasive argument.

PAGES 12–13

Task: Give tips on learning a language well

Common European Framework: Students can develop an argument systematically with appropriate highlighting of significant points, and relevant supporting detail.

PAGES 14–15

Writing: A report

Listening: Varieties of English

Pronunciation: Varieties of English

Common European Framework: Students can write a report that develops an argument systematically with appropriate highlighting of significant points and relevant supporting detail; can understand a wide range of recorded and broadcast audio material.

Vocabulary and speaking (PAGES 6–7)

Globalisation

See *Teaching tips: Working with lexis*, page 21.

WARM UP

Write the following questions on the board:

What is your country famous for?

What do people from other countries usually think about people from your country?

Has this changed at all over the past ten years?

How often do you speak to people from other countries?

Students discuss the questions in small groups. In feedback, elicit students' ideas and have a brief class discussion.

1a Focus students on the photos and elicit some ideas about what they can see. Elicit some ideas about what globalisation is, e.g. the process by which countries become connected or similar, especially because large companies are doing business in many different countries. Go through the example with the class and give students one minute to think about how globalisation affects them. Go around and help with vocabulary where necessary.

b Nominate students to share their ideas with the class.

2 Check understanding of the things in the list, especially *lingua franca* (a language people whose first languages are different use to communicate) and *webinars* (live workshops and lectures streamed over the internet). Model the activity by telling students about one of the things you've experienced, sharing details about what happened and what you found interesting. Students then discuss their own experiences in groups.

3 With weaker classes, go through the phrases first and check understanding. Students discuss the question in groups. In feedback, nominate one student from each group to share their ideas with the class, and check understanding of the phrases where necessary.

4 Read the example with the class. Students add the words/phrases to the word web alone then check in pairs. While students are doing this, you can make a note of any pronunciation problems to focus on in feedback, e.g. the stress on *diversity* (.●..) and the pronunciation of *culture* (/'kʌltʃə/).

ANSWERS:

travel: immigration/emigration, mass tourism

food: imported, local produce

business/money: international conference calls, webinars, immigration/emigration, multinational corporations, imported, higher standard of living, brain drain, sweatshops, global financial crises, global brands

communication/language: online contact, lingua franca

shopping: multinational corporations, imported, local produce, global brands

culture/society: cultural and religious diversity, races, way of life, a clash of cultures, a multi-ethnic society, Americanised, higher standard of living, brain drain

---

5 Encourage students to use the vocabulary from exercise 3 in their lists of advantages and disadvantages, e.g. an advantage is that you can choose from a variety of ethnic restaurants when you go out to eat.

6a 🎧 1.1 Go through the questions with the class and check students understand what to listen for.

b Give students a chance to compare answers in pairs before going through the answers. Play the recording a second time if necessary.

ANSWERS:

1 Speaker 1: the world is a smaller place and things are more accessible; we can share ideas and this creates a sense of tolerance

Speaker 2: towns are identical because shops are the same; it makes things bland

Speaker 3: people are more tolerant because there are people from different countries living together

Speaker 4: you can see the same movies everywhere; this means that independent movies sometimes suffer

Speaker 5: you can have a variety of food

Speaker 6: places which don't have much internet access, or multinational companies, like Cuba, can keep their identity

2 Speaker 1: for

Speaker 2: against

Speaker 3: for

Speaker 4: mixed feelings

Speaker 5: for

Speaker 6: mixed feelings

---

c While students are looking at the audio script, go around and answer any questions. In feedback, write the words/phrases on the board and check understanding and pronunciation.

7 Give students a few minutes in pairs to think how to explain the differences. You could make this into a competition by giving points, e.g. a point for the best explanation, for accurate pronunciation, for using one of the words/phrases accurately in an example sentence.

ANSWERS:

1 emigration = to leave your own country in order to live in another one
immigration = the process of entering another country in order to live there

2 multinational = a company which has factories, offices and business activities in many different countries
multi-ethnic = involving or including people of several different ethnic groups

3 cultural diversity = including many different types of people or things
a clash of cultures = a conflict arising from two or more different cultural groups being in close proximity to one another

4 a business = an organisation which produces or sells goods or provides a service
a corporation = a big company or a group of companies

5 your standard of living = the amount of wealth, comfort and other things that a particular person, group, country, etc. has
your way of life = the behaviour, habits, customs, etc. that are typical of a particular society or person

> **Vocabulary and speaking, exercise 7: Alternative suggestion**
> Before class, write the words/phrases on ten separate pieces of paper, and make enough sets for one per group of three to four students. Put students into groups and hand out one set per group. Students match the pairs of similar words/phrases, then discuss how they are different.

ADDITIONAL PRACTICE

➡ **Resource bank:** Activity 1C *Global village* (Globalisation)

Vocabulary practice: Exercise 1

Workbook: Vocabulary: *Globalisation*, page 4

Reading and vocabulary (PAGES 8–9)

Urbanisation

See *Teaching tips: Working with lexis*, page 21.

1 Write the following words on the board: *housing, shops, traffic, crime, green areas*. Give students a minute to think about the changes related to the topics before discussing in pairs. In feedback, nominate students to share their ideas with the class.

2a Students work alone to read and mark the words/phrases. Don't give any answers yet.

b When students have finished comparing, check understanding of the words/phrases by eliciting examples in the local area. Check pronunciation of the phrases, especially the stress on *availability* (•••●••), *sprawl* (/sprɔːl/) and *infrastructure* (/ˈɪnfrəstrʌktʃə/).

3a Elicit students' ideas then give the answers. If possible, show where they are on a map of the world.

ANSWERS:
Washington DC – the USA
Dhaka – Bangladesh
Songdo – South Korea
Medellin – Colombia

b Students read the text and answer the questions alone, then check in pairs. Check answers with the whole class.

ANSWERS:
1 Humans recently became an 'urban species' – more people live in cities than in the countryside.
2 Cities were not originally designed to cope with a growing number of people, and there is a limited amount of housing available.
3 Le Corbusier proposed demolishing the centre of Paris to make way for high-rise buildings.

4 Elicit the first answer as an example. Students find the phrases then check in pairs. With weaker classes, you could give them the paragraphs which the phrases appear in (paragraph 1: 1–3, paragraph 2: 4–6, paragraph 3: 7–8, paragraph 4: 9).

ANSWERS:
1 ... this global trend is heading ever upwards.
2 The speed and scale of this change is unprecedented ...
3 ... fast-growing cities bring with them numerous issues ...
4 That's an awful lot of people to fit into such a small space and most cities just weren't designed to cope.
5 ... limited availability and unlimited demand are driving property prices sky-high.
6 So what, if anything, can be done about urbanisation?
7 ... and designer Le Corbusier was no exception.
8 He devised a plan ... to demolish the centre of Paris ...
9 Demolishing and rebuilding cities to meet modern needs is clearly impractical ...

5 Elicit/Check: *from scratch* (from nothing), *tubes* (round pipes used to carry liquid or gas), *initiatives* (ideas, projects) and *crèche* (a place where babies / small children can be left for a short while, e.g. while the parents go to work). Put students into pairs to read the texts. Before they read, tell students that afterwards they'll summarise their text for their partner, so they should take notes while they read.

6a Students share information in pairs.

b Students discuss the questions in pairs. In feedback, nominate students to share their ideas with the class and have a brief class discussion.

ADDITIONAL PRACTICE

➡ **Resource bank:** Activity 1D *Picture this* (Urbanisation)

Vocabulary practice: Exercise 2

Workbook: Vocabulary: *Urbanisation*, page 4; Listen and read: *City or country?*, pages 4–5

Grammar review (PAGE 9)

Continuous verb forms

See *Teaching tips: Using a discovery approach to grammar*, page 20.

1a–b Focus attention on the sentences and elicit the answers to the questions. Emphasise that continuous forms are often used to focus on the action rather than the result.

> **ANSWERS:**
> **1a** In sentence 1, the writer is more interested in the result. In sentence 2, the writer is more interested in the action in progress.
> **b** When the focus is on the action, the continuous form is used.

2 Students work alone then check in pairs. Check that students understand how to form the continuous aspect in different tenses by eliciting more examples.

> **ANSWERS:**
> 1 the Present perfect continuous
> 2 a simple form; the Future continuous
> 3 the Present continuous
> 4 the Present continuous
> 5 a continuous passive

3a Go through the example with the class. Students work in pairs to match the ideas with the examples from exercise 2.

> **ANSWERS:**
> **b** 2: ... by 2050, seven billion of us will be living in an urban environment.
> **c** 4: This global trend is heading ever upwards.
> **d** 1: Humans have been building cities for nine millennia.
> **e** 5: ... plans are in the process of being drawn up ...

b Answer the question as a class.

> **ANSWER:**
> *Believe* can't be used in the continuous form because it is a state verb, and we use continuous forms when the focus is on the action. Other examples of state verbs include *know, be, appear* and *like*.

You may want to ask students to read Language summary 1 on pages 112–113 for a more detailed explanation of continuous verb forms.

4 Choose two of the sentences and give examples about yourself. While students are completing the sentences, go around and help with vocabulary, writing any new words/phrases on the board. When they are ready, students share their ideas in pairs.

> **Grammar review, exercise 4: Alternative suggestion**
> When students have completed the sentences, they take it in turns to read out just the part they've completed to their partner, who listens and guesses which sentence they are completing.

ADDITIONAL PRACTICE

➡ **Resource bank:** Activity 1A *What are you doing?* (Continuous verb forms)

Grammar practice: Exercises 1–8

Workbook: Grammar: *Continuous verb forms*, pages 6–7

Listening and speaking (PAGES 10–11)

English in a changing world

1 This stage need only be a brief lead in and could be skipped, so you start the section with exercise 2a.

2a Students work in pairs, then as a whole class, taking votes on which two pieces of information are false.

b Students discuss the question in pairs. In feedback, elicit students' ideas.

3 You could do the first example with the whole class, finding out how many people agree/disagree with or are not sure about the statement. After students have compared answers, ask one or two groups to report back briefly on their ideas.

4 🎧 **1.2** Suggest that students use a different colour pen to mark Doctor Jenkins' answers next to their own for the statements in exercise 3.

> **ANSWERS:**
> **agrees:**
> 5 majority of people who speak English around the world are non-native speakers, they use it to communicate with each other
> 6 people have the right to develop their own ways of speaking; speakers of English should 'be themselves'
> **disagrees:**
> 1 non-native speakers of English are in the majority
> 2 speakers of international English need to be intelligible to each other, not aim for 'perfect' speech
> 3 British and American idioms are not used for international communication
> 4 some grammar usage which would be regarded as incorrect, will become the 'norm' in international English

5a–b Focus students on the language areas in the list and elicit some ideas about the areas they find most problematic (e.g. always forgetting to put the third person *-s* in the Present simple – none of the other persons change, which seems to make it more difficult to remember). Give students a few minutes to discuss the other language areas in pairs before playing the recording again.

> **ANSWERS:**
> • *th-* will be pronounced as /s/ or /t/
> • British and American idioms will not be used
> • uncountable nouns like *information* will be countable (e.g. 'three informations')
> • the third person *-s* will not be used

6a This can be done as a whole class discussion. Keep the discussion quite brief, so that student interest is maintained for the next stage.

b Give students a few minutes in small groups to think of their questions, referring them back to the statements in exercise 3 and the language areas in exercise 5a, as well as their notes from exercise 5b. When you answer the students' questions, speak naturally and at some length if you want to: this is a good opportunity for students to practise 'live' listening, i.e. as they listen to you.

PATTERNS TO NOTICE

Introducing points in an argument

1 🎧 1.3 Students listen to the extracts and complete the sentences. Answer the question as a class and drill the phrases.

ANSWERS:

1 Well, there are two things. One thing is that they're intelligible to each other.
2 The second thing would be that nobody owns English any more.
3 One advantage would be that learners have less to do.

The introductory phrases add a clear structure and organisation to the argument, making it easy to understand.

2 Give students time to look at the other examples and discuss in pairs which are for and against an argument, and which could be either.

ANSWERS:

Introducing points for an argument:
Another (strong) reason (for) …
The main explanation …

Introducing points against an argument:
The most (obvious) drawback/advantage (of) …
The second problem/concern/issue (with) …

Either:
One (important) point to consider …
A further consideration …

Pronunciation: Helping students with sentence stress

To help students with the phrases for introducing points in an argument, say some examples at natural speed but with slightly exaggerated stress, and see if students can hear where the stress falls. The tendency is for the main stress to fall on the 'key' information in the phrase:

Well, there are two points to consider. One point is that …
The second point would be that …
Another issue might be that …

Get students to repeat these examples, then get them to make more phrases from the substitution table in exercise 2 and say them aloud.

---

7 If necessary, do the first one as an example. Students work alone then check in pairs, before checking answers with the whole class.

ANSWERS:

1 The main point to consider would be that …
2 A further advantage of Global English is that …
3 One possible problem with British English or American English might be that …
4 The most obvious reason for pronunciation problems is that …

8 Students complete the phrases alone then check in pairs.

9a–b Decide how long you will give students to think about what to say: this could be as little as ten seconds if you want to increase the pressure to speak spontaneously. You can also regulate the pressure by getting students to speak in front of the whole class or in smaller groups.

Listening and speaking, exercise 9: Alternative suggestion

To add an element of competition, run this as a game of 'Just a minute', where a student has to try to keep talking on the topic for a minute, but others in the group can interrupt him/her for hesitation, repetition or mistakes in English. The person who made the interruption then has to continue speaking for what is left of the minute, and so on. The person speaking at the end of the minute is the winner.

ADDITIONAL PRACTICE

➡ **Resource bank:** Activity 1B *You've got a point* (Introducing points in an argument)

Workbook: Grammar: *Introducing points in an argument*, page 7

Task (PAGES 12–13)

Give tips on learning a language well

See *Teaching tips: Making tasks work*, page 23.

WARM UP

Write the following on the board:
remember new words, use grammar correctly, improve pronunciation, practise listening and speaking, practise writing, improve reading

In pairs, students discuss how they do each of the things on the board in English. When they have finished, elicit students' ideas and write them on the board as word webs for each area.

Preparation (PAGES 12–13)

Listening and reading

1 🎧 1.4 Focus attention on the questions and check students know what to listen for. Students listen to the recording then check answers in pairs. If necessary, play the recording again. In feedback, write the strategies on the board for students to refer to in exercise 2.

ANSWERS:

Speaker 1: English; watching films and TV with the subtitles; she enjoyed the film and didn't feel like she was learning

Speaker 2: Spanish; doing a class in tango guitar; it helps the language sink in

Speaker 3: English; try to think in English and imagine conversations

Speaker 4: English; put the radio / YouTube on in the background while doing something else; English in the background was really helpful

Speaker 5: get a girlfriend from the country of the language you wish to learn; you have to communicate constantly in that language

Speaker 6: English; talk to everybody

Speaker 7: Spanish; read things online that you are interested in; it's great for vocabulary

2 Students read the profiles and take notes on the people's needs and possible strategies to help.

ANSWERS:

Adriana: needs to use English on a daily basis, answer the phone, speak to English-speaking colleagues and attend meetings in English.

David: needs to improve German communication skills quickly.

Kareem: needs to read fluently in English and dramatically improve his vocabulary. Also needs to understand lectures and socialise.

Asha: wants to maintain and improve her Russian.

Akiko: needs to improve listening and speaking, and improve her confidence in using English.

Listening and reading, exercise 2: Alternative suggestion

Do this as a jigsaw reading activity. Put students into two groups. Ask one group to read Adriana's and David's profiles and make notes. Ask the other group to read Kareem's, Asha's and Akiko's profiles and make notes. When they have finished, rearrange students into pairs, with one student from each of the groups to share the information they read about.

Task (PAGES 12–13)

Speaking

1 Go through the phrases in the Useful language box, section a. Put students into groups to think of additional tips. Go around and help with vocabulary where necessary, writing any new words/phrases on the board.

2 Ask each group to choose a representative to share their ideas with the class. As they share ideas, build a list of strategies on the board or ask a student to do so.

3a Refer students to the phrases in the Useful language box, section b and then ask them to discuss the questions in pairs.

b You could encourage students to keep a journal, writing a brief entry every day that they try the strategy, before reporting back in a few weeks' time.

Task: Additional suggestion

Students write about the best strategies they've used in the past, following the model of the speakers in Preparation, exercise 1.

Share your task

Some additional ideas could include:

- Students just film/record themselves talking about their needs and motivation. Other students then watch/listen to the recordings and give tips.
- Students film/record themselves giving their best three tips for learning English. Other students then watch/listen to the recordings and decide which they like best.
- Students keep a video/audio log of their progress trying out the two tips from exercise 3b. After two weeks, they then share the recordings with other students and decide which of the tips have been most useful.

Language live (PAGES 14–15)

Writing (PAGES 14–15)

A report

WARM UP

Bring/Download logos from global brand cafés and restaurants (e.g. *McDonald's*, *KFC*, *Starbucks*, *Subway*, *Pizza Hut*, *Dunkin' Donuts*, *Hard Rock Café*, etc.). Put students into teams, and show the logos, one by one, asking students to write the name of the café or restaurant in their teams. When you have shown all of them, check students' answers, and award points for each correct one. The team with the most points wins.

1a If you did the Warm up activity, then skip this and go straight to exercise 1b. Students discuss in pairs. When they are ready, elicit their ideas and write them on the board, and add *Starbucks*, *Subway* and *Hard Rock Café* if students have not included them.

b Students discuss the questions in pairs. In feedback, nominate students to share their ideas with the class.

2a Give students a few minutes to read the report and find similarities with their town / local area.

b Students work alone then check in pairs. In feedback, be prepared to give further explanations/examples of how the linking words are used where necessary.

ANSWERS:

1 also   2 Although / Even though   3 As well as / Apart from
4 as well as that / other than that / apart from that
5 on the other hand   6 Just/Only   7 while/whereas
8 even if / although   9 this means that / this explains why

---

3 Students work in pairs to compile their lists. Encourage them to find examples in the report on page 14. In feedback, elicit their ideas and write them on the board.

ANSWERS:

an introduction and a conclusion; clear, simple headings

4a Put students into groups to discuss the ideas in the word web. In monolingual classes, you could discuss the question as a class, asking students for examples of each of the things in the word web.

b Encourage students to make notes, as this will help when they come to write their reports. Monitor and help with vocabulary where necessary, writing any new words/phrases on the board.

5 Elicit an example and write it on the board. Go around while students are writing their sentences and check they are forming them correctly.

6a Give students plenty of time to organise and write the first draft of their reports, and go around and help where necessary.

b Students check their own work, then discuss their corrections with their partner. When they have finished, display their reports around the class and ask other students to walk around and read them, choosing which they find most interesting.

Listening (PAGE 15)

Varieties of English

See *Teaching tips: Helping students with pronunciation*, page 22.

1a 🎧 1.5 Introduce the topic by asking students which English accents they are most familiar with, and which they find most difficult to understand. Elicit where English is spoken around the world. Students listen and answer the questions in pairs.

Potential problem with unfamiliar accents

Students are likely to find it difficult to follow accents which they aren't familiar with. Try to put them at ease here and explain that by practising listening to unfamiliar accents they'll be able to understand them quite quickly, as they already know much of the language.

---

b Students listen again and note down the numbers and statistics, then check in pairs. Go through answers with the class by writing the numbers on the board and asking what they refer to.

ANSWERS:

Report 1: A hurricane in the US: tens of thousands of people evacuating; clean-up could cost over $15 billion; Hurricane Katrina cost $100 billion in 2005. The storm affects financial markets across the world.

Report 2: A Japanese company is creating jobs in the UK: there will be 200 new jobs; the factory has been manufacturing cars for more than 25 years; a local firm will close, losing 150 jobs. The story concerns the effect of multinational corporations on local businesses.

Report 3: Attitudes to climate change among Australians: the vast majority think that climate change is happening; two-thirds believe that countries like the US and China are responsible; these two countries create over 12,000 million tonnes of greenhouse gases per year. The story concerns the global effects of industry and pollution.

Report 4: A Starbucks opens in Mumbai, India: the company has 20,000 branches in more than 60 countries. The story concerns global brands and franchises.

---

2 Play the recording again for students to listen to the accents. You do not need to go into detail here – just see if students can get a general impression of the differences.

3a–b 🎧 **1.6** How much time you spend on this will depend on your students' interest and their listening abilities. They may find it interesting/amusing to try to hear the differences and imitate the accents from the recording. With stronger classes, you could ask individual students to imitate an accent for other students to guess which it is.

POSSIBLE ANSWERS:

American English: 'r' sound is stronger than in British English; 't' in words like *duty* sounds more like 'd'.

Indian English: 'd' is softer than in British English; 'r' is more rolled; 'l' is stronger; 't' is softer and sounds more like 'd'. The intonation is more musical.

Australian English: 'a' sound in words like *past* and 'i' sound in words like *night* and *lives* is longer than in British English. The differences are less distinct than the other accents, except for the rising intonation at the end of sentences.

4 Students discuss the questions in pairs. In feedback, elicit their ideas and have a class discussion.

ADDITIONAL PRACTICE

➡ **Workbook:** Writing: *Linking words and phrases* and *Useful phrases for report writing*, page 8; Language live: *Varieties of English*, page 8

Grammar practice (PAGES 114–115)

See *Teaching tips: Using the Grammar and Vocabulary practice sections*, page 25.

Continuous verb forms

ANSWERS:

1

I'm sitting in a café; *(I'm) waiting to meet*; *he's bending down* – situations happening around a point of time

I was getting more depressed ... every day – involving change or development

he's been working really hard – situation happening over a period of time

it seems to be paying off – emphasises that the action is in progress now

who are now enjoying – happening over a period of time in the present

I'd been going on dates – happening over a period of time in the past

I was always turning up; *the guy was constantly planning* – something that happens regularly, and was irritating

I've been going on a few dates; *it's been going really well* – incomplete

2

1 been arguing **2** been playing **3** finished **4** been thinking **5** been watching, done **6** seen **7** left **8** been doing

3

1 follows **2** have been putting on **3** have been working **4** enjoy **5** have been learning **6** struggle **7** are helping

5

1 Jo's eyes seem to be getting worse. / c
2 You're always losing your mobile phone. / f
3 Are you coming to the work party? / a
4 I was hoping you could help me with my homework. / b
5 I was wondering if you'd like to go to the cinema. / d
6 We were wondering if you could feed our cat while we're on holiday. / e

6

2 ... – she must be working from home.
3 You can't still be getting ready ...
4 ... I'd like to be sitting ...
6 You seem to be spending ...
7 He's bound to be watching TV.
8 He's supposed to be tidying ...
10 He seems to be doing well ...

7

1 i n ('look' is a state verb, and means 'appear');
ii h ('looking' describes an action, and is similar in meaning to 'watch')
2 i d ('feel' is a state verb, and describes how I feel in general in these clothes);
ii c ('feeling' describes an active feeling in progress)
3 i a ('having' describes an action, and means 'eating');
ii l ('have' is a state verb, used to describe possession)
4 i g ('fit' is a state verb, and means 'be the right size');
ii k ('fitting' describes an action, and means 'installing')
5 i e ('expecting' describes an action, and means 'waiting for');
ii i ('expect' is a state verb, and means 'imagine')
6 i f ('admire' is a state verb, and means 'have a good opinion of');
ii m ('admiring' describes an action, and means 'looking at with appreciation')
7 i b ('thinking' describes an action, and means 'considering');
ii j ('think' is a state verb, and means 'suppose/guess')

8

1 was looking **2** 's having **3** are seeing
4 are you feeling / do you feel **5** Are you expecting
6 are you measuring, fits **7** appeared

Vocabulary practice (PAGE 152)

Globalisation

ANSWERS:

1

1 Americanised **2** sweatshops **3** way of life **4** global brand
5 brain drain **6** local produce **7** clash of cultures
8 multinational corporations

Urbanisation

ANSWERS:

2

1 green belt land **2** no-go areas **3** reclaimed land **4** slums
5 squalor **6** congestion

Other words and phrases

ANSWERS:

3

1 brand new **2** keep up with **3** scale
4 being used as a template **5** side effect **6** from scratch
7 bold **8** drew up

OVERVIEW

PAGES 16–17

Vocabulary and speaking: Feelings

Pronunciation: Stress patterns in single-word adjectives

Common European Framework: Students can give clear, detailed descriptions; can vary intonation and place sentence stress correctly.

PAGES 18–19

Reading: Expressing emotions across the world

Grammar review: Perfect verb forms

Common European Framework: Students can understand articles and reports concerned with contemporary problems in which the writers adopt particular stances or viewpoints; can identify unfamiliar words from the context.

PAGES 20–21

Listening and vocabulary: Advertising and emotions

Patterns to notice: Cleft sentences

Wordspot: Idioms with *laugh*, *cry* and *tears*

Common European Framework: Students can understand a wide range of recorded and broadcast audio material; have a good command of idiomatic expressions.

PAGES 22–23

Task: Describe a story that provokes strong emotions

Common European Framework: Students can give elaborate descriptions and narratives.

PAGES 24–25

World culture: Luxury superbrands

Common European Framework: Students can follow extended speech even when it is not clearly structured and when relationships are only implied and not signalled explicitly; can summarise information from different sources in a coherent presentation.

Vocabulary and speaking

(PAGES 16–17)

Feelings

See *Teaching tips: Working with lexis*, page 21.

WARM UP

Explain to the class that you are going to do a word association activity. You will say an emotion, and students must listen and write down the first thing they can think of that they associate with that feeling. Ask them to write their words in random order. Read out the following words, pausing after each one for students to write something, and write each word on the board after you've said it: *happy*, *relaxed*, *shocked*, *depressed*, *scared*, *excited*, *embarrassed*, *nervous*.

Put students into pairs to show each other what they wrote. Their partner tries to guess which emotion on the board each word is related to.

1a Go through the words/phrases with the class, checking understanding by eliciting situations in which a person might feel that way. Check pronunciation, especially the stress in *devastated* (●●●●), *apprehensive* (●●●●●) and *disillusioned* (●●●●●). Students discuss the photos in pairs, before sharing their ideas with the whole class.

b Discuss this question with the whole class.

2 Students discuss in pairs. In feedback, elicit any other adjectives they've thought of and write them on the board.

> **ANSWERS:**
> The following words express particularly strong emotions: ashamed; desperate; devastated; disgusted; helpless; overjoyed; scared stiff; mortified; shattered.

3 Elicit/Check: *pass with flying colours* (pass really well, with a good result/grade), *incoherent* (impossible to understand), *sniggering* (laughing in a nasty way) and *out of the blue* (suddenly). Put students into groups to read the situations then discuss how they'd feel. In feedback, nominate a student from each group to share their ideas with the class.

4a Read the example with the class, and if necessary do another one as an example. Students complete the chart alone then check in pairs.

b 🎧 **2.1** Play the recording for students to check their answers. Play it a second time for students to practise saying the words.

> **ANSWERS:**
> **1** desperate, helpless, shattered   **2** ashamed, relieved
> **3** envious, mortified   **4** disgusted, indifferent
> **5** insecure, overjoyed   **6** devastated   **7** apprehensive, disillusioned

5a Give students plenty of time to invent situations in pairs. Encourage them to think about them and/or take notes rather than write a full description. Monitor and help with vocabulary, writing any new words/phrases on the board.

b When they are ready, pairs describe their situations for the class to guess the emotions. With large classes, you could join pairs into groups of four.

ADDITIONAL PRACTICE

➡ **Resource bank:** Activity 2C *How does it feel?* (Feelings)

Vocabulary practice: Exercise 1

Workbook: Vocabulary: *Feelings*, page 9; Pronunciation: *Word stress*, page 9

Reading (PAGES 18–19)

Expressing emotions across the world

1 Introduce the topic by telling the class about some of the things that you've done recently and why you did them. Put students into groups to share their ideas.

2a Elicit/Check: *sweltering* (very hot and humid), *grasp* (understand), *slam the door* (shut the door loudly and violently), *strained smile* (a false smile which hides a negative feeling) and *sulk* (be in a bad mood because you can't get what you want). Give students one minute to read the first paragraph, then discuss the question in pairs. Check answers with the class.

b Ask students to read the full article quickly to find the answers to the questions. Explain they will have a chance to read it again more carefully afterwards. Students check answers in pairs before checking with the whole class.

> **ANSWERS:**
> **1** negativity, whinging and whining (complaining), anger
> **2** There are subtle ways to express strong emotions, through a variety of smiles. The eyes can also convey a lot of different emotions.
> **3** **Arun:** doesn't like the way Americans show conflicts; finds some people's behaviour dishonest
> **Karly:** likes the South-East Asian way of smiling and being calm and laid-back
> **Andreas:** doesn't think it's good for people to bottle up their anger

3 Students read the article again and decide which statements are not true. In pairs, they compare which parts of the article give the answers before checking with the whole class.

ANSWERS:
1 T ('I thought he was joking at first')
2 T ('people go out of their way to put on a happy face')
3 F ('in collective cultures like Thailand's')
4 T ('In ... Europe or the USA, it is relatively common for friends and partners to have a brief slanging match')
5 F ('That is not to say you can't express negative emotions in Thailand')
6 T ('I try to tone down my behaviour')
7 T ('A flatmate from Italy used to tell me how uptight I was')
8 F ('Personally, it would drive me nuts!')

4 Encourage students to use the context and surrounding words to help them guess the meanings. In feedback, elicit answers and be prepared to give further examples/explanations where necessary.

POSSIBLE ANSWERS:
1 complaining
2 arguing, fighting using words
3 become angry, lose your temper
4 reduce an aspect of your behaviour
5 be unable to relax
6 be calm and relaxed
7 keep your feelings hidden
8 make someone upset or angry

5 Put students into groups to discuss the questions. In feedback, nominate a student from each group to share their answers with the class and have a brief class discussion.

6 Ask students if they ever leave comments after reading articles or blogs, and what kind of comments they leave. Ask students to write their own comment on a separate piece of paper. Monitor and help with ideas and vocabulary where necessary. When they have finished, collect the comments and display them around the classroom. Ask students to walk around and read the other comments, then ask them which they like best.

ADDITIONAL PRACTICE
➡ **Workbook:** Listen and read: *A tale of two countries*, page 10

Grammar review (PAGE 19)

Perfect verb forms

See *Teaching tips: Using a discovery approach to grammar*, page 20.

1 Students read the comment and note the country and cultural problems. Check answers with the class.

ANSWERS:
Indonesia; standing with hands on hips, sitting and showing the soles of the feet, touching people's heads

2 The aim of this exercise is to give you a chance to assess how much students know about perfect verb forms. Elicit how we form the perfect aspect (auxiliary *have* + past participle). Students underline the perfect verb forms, then discuss why each one is used in pairs.

ANSWERS:
a we've been caught out (Present perfect simple – the writer is looking back at repeated experiences in the past up to the present time)
b I'd been standing (Past perfect continuous – the writer is describing a past time action which happened before 'people sometimes gave me angry looks'; the continuous is used here to describe an activity which took place over a period of time)
c we've had to learn (Present perfect simple – the writer is looking back from the present time to the time when he moved to Jakarta)
d to have known (perfect infinitive – the writer is looking back from a point in the past to a point further in the past)
e we've all been trying (Present perfect continuous – the writer is describing repeated experiences in the recent past up to now)
f we will have been (Future perfect – the writer is looking back into the past from a point in the future)
g it's been (Present perfect simple – the writer is describing experiences in the recent past up to now)

3a Students answer the questions alone, then check in pairs before checking answers with the whole class.

ANSWERS:
1 c (*since* links a point in the past to the present)
2 g (*so far* indicates that the period is incomplete)
3 a (*several times* shows that this has happened various times)
4 e   5 b   6 f   7 d

b Explain that all perfect forms aim to link two times together. With weaker classes, you could direct them to the timelines in the Language summary on page 116 if you think they would benefit from seeing this visually. Students answer the questions using the forms given in exercise 3a, then check in pairs. Check answers with the whole class.

ANSWERS:
the past and present: Present perfect
two points in the past: Past perfect
two points in the future: Future perfect

Potential problem with the perfect aspect

Many students find the perfect aspect difficult, even at advanced level, as it doesn't exist in their first language (or is rarely used). It's important therefore to give a 'global' view of the perfect aspect, i.e. that it always links two time periods, in order to help make it clearer.

You may want to ask students to read Language summary 2 on pages 116–117 for a more detailed explanation of perfect verb forms.

4 Give students a few minutes to complete the sentences. Go around and check they have formed the perfect verb forms correctly. When they are ready, put students into groups to discuss which sentences are true for them.

ANSWERS:
1 've been working   2 've studied   3 'll have found out
4 to have started   5 haven't had   6 'd been talking

ADDITIONAL PRACTICE
➡ **Resource bank:** Activity 2A *Me too!* (Perfect verb forms)
Grammar practice: Exercises 1–9
Workbook: Grammar: *Perfect verb forms*, page 11

Listening and vocabulary (PAGES 20–21)

Advertising and emotions

WARM UP

Bring/Download a variety of adverts. Try to find a range of different types (for example those in exercise 2a). Show them to the class, and ask students to discuss which they like/dislike and why in pairs.

1 Focus attention on the photos and elicit what students can see. Elicit/ Teach the different words for *advertisement* in English, i.e. *ad* or *advert*, and *commercial* for TV. Students discuss the questions in groups. In feedback, elicit students' ideas and have a brief class discussion.

2a Do the first one together as an example. Students then read and mark the rest of the statements on their own.

b 🎧 2.2 Elicit/Check: *under the bonnet* (in the engine) and *kudos* (respect). Play the recording for students to check their answers.

ANSWERS:

1 R 2 R 3 E 4 E 5 R 6 E 7 E 8 E

3a Give students a few minutes to read the sentences and answer any questions they have about the words, providing further examples/ explanations where necessary. When they are ready, play the recording again for students to decide if the sentences are true or false.

b Students compare their answers in pairs before checking with the whole class. When going through the answers, ask students to give reasons for their answers.

ANSWERS:

1 T 2 F 3 T 4 F 5 T 6 F 7 F 8 F 9 T 10 T

4 Students discuss the questions in groups.

Listening and vocabulary, exercise 4: Alternative suggestion

Put students into pairs to find specific examples of adverts online which have the messages in exercise 2a. When they are ready, join pairs into groups of four. Students show each other their adverts for the other pair to guess which of the messages in exercise 2a each one shows.

PATTERNS TO NOTICE

Cleft sentences

1 🎧 2.3 Students work in pairs to complete the sentences, then listen to the recording and check their answers.

ANSWERS:

1 What most people prefer is straightforward facts.
2 It's often charity ads that appeal to 'negative' emotions.

2 Focus attention on the examples. Students answer the questions in pairs before checking answers with the whole class.

ANSWERS:

1 In the second (cleft) sentences, the information that is emphasised always comes after the verb *be*, i.e.
It wasn't me ...   *It was then* ...
What you should do is tell her the truth.
What I like (about her) is the way she smiles.
2 If we want to focus on a person, a time, etc., we use a cleft sentence starting with an *it* clause. If we want to focus on an idea or an action, we use a cleft sentence starting with a *what* clause.
3 With *it* clauses, we put *be* after *it*. With *what* clauses, we put *be* at the end of the clause.
4 *It* clauses are followed by a relative pronoun.

---

5 Elicit the first answer as an example, then students rewrite the rest of the sentences alone. In feedback, ask a different student to come to the board and write each cleft sentence.

ANSWERS:

1 What you need is a few days' rest and recreation.
2 It's money that people care about most nowadays.
3 What we need is someone to help us, not someone to criticise.
4 What I like (about him) is the way he always listens sympathetically.
5 It's his attitude towards other people that really annoys me.
6 What I don't understand is why you had to lie to me.
7 It wasn't me who decided to take a short cut across country!
8 What the world needs is love, peace and understanding.
9 It was then that everything became clear.

Listening and vocabulary, exercise 5: Alternative suggestion

Books closed. Put students into two teams, and give each team a board pen. For each item, write the word in brackets on the board and read out the original sentence. Someone from each team then comes to the board and writes the cleft sentence. The first team to write it correctly wins a point, and the team with the most points wins. If you are using an IWB, then teams can write the sentences on a piece of paper and hold it up when they've finished.

---

6 Give students a few minutes to complete the sentences. Go around and help with vocabulary where necessary, writing any new words/phrases on the board.

ADDITIONAL PRACTICE

➡ **Resource bank:** Activity 2B *What I want to say is* ... (Cleft sentences)
   Workbook: Vocabulary: *Advertising and emotions*, page 12; Grammar: *Cleft sentences*, page 12

Wordspot (PAGE 21)

Idioms with *laugh*, *cry* and *tears*

See *Teaching tips: Working with lexis*, page 21.

1a Write *laugh*, *cry* and *tears* on the board and check pronunciation and understanding. Elicit any idioms students know with these words and write them on the board. Students try to complete the sentences in pairs. Encourage them to use their mobile phones to search for the idioms if they have them.

ANSWERS:

1 cry (someone who gives you sympathy)
2 tears ('floods' suggests a lot of tears)
3 laugh (to be successful in the end after people have doubted or criticised you)
4 cry   5 tears   6 laugh   7 laugh
8 tears (the verb 'burst' in 7 and 8 means that the laughing or crying started suddenly)
9 laugh   10 tears

Wordspot, exercise 1a: Alternative suggestion

Books closed. Put students into teams, and ask each team to write the words *laugh*, *cry* and *tears* on three separate pieces of paper. Each turn, read out one of the gapped phrases in exercise 1a. Students raise the paper with the missing word to complete the idiom. The first team to raise the correct word wins a point, and the team with the most points wins. After the game, students complete the phrases in their books in pairs.

---

b Focus attention on the cartoons and elicit which idioms are shown.

ANSWERS:

left: laugh your head off

right: be in floods of tears

2a–b Students can do this individually or in pairs when checking their answers.

ANSWERS:

1 It's no laughing matter.
2 in floods of tears / crying her eyes out
3 had the last laugh
4 burst into tears
5 a shoulder to cry on
6 laughed his head off
7 burst out laughing
8 close to tears
9 was in floods of tears / cried my eyes out
10 bored to tears

> **Wordspot, exercise 2: Alternative suggestion**
>
> Students 'test' each other in pairs: student A closes his/her book and student B reads out some of the sentences, stopping before the phrase in bold, and prompting student A to complete the sentence with the appropriate idiom, e.g. *I'm not sure you realise just how serious the parking problem is around here. ... ?* Then students swap roles.

3 Give students a few minutes to prepare before putting them in groups to share their ideas. You could ask them to describe the situation for others to guess which idiom they are describing. In feedback, nominate students to share their ideas with the class.

ADDITIONAL PRACTICE

➡ **Resource bank:** Activity 2D *Once upon a time* (Idioms with *laugh*, *cry* and *tears*)

Vocabulary practice: Exercise 2

Workbook: Wordspot: *Idioms with* laugh, cry *and* tears, page 13

Task (PAGES 22–23)

Describe a story that provokes strong emotions

See *Teaching tips: Making tasks work*, page 23.

Preparation (PAGE 22)

Listening and speaking

1a Introduce the topic by telling the class about books, films or plays that have made you feel that way. Give students a few minutes to think of their own examples.

b Put students into groups to share their ideas.

2 Students discuss in pairs. In feedback, encourage them to give an example of each and find out if other students agree.

3a 🎧 **2.4** Before they listen, go through the questions with the whole class and check understanding of the words/phrases in the box. If possible, set students up in separate rooms to listen to the stories at the same time. If not, then the two groups can listen to the stories one after the other. After they have listened, students compare answers in their group.

ANSWERS:

Story A
1 The Tell-Tale Heart (from a short story)
2 America, the 1840s
3 a thriller / murder story
4 in detail
5 an old man and a murderer
6 police interview, floorboards, heart beating, insane narrator, scream

Story B
1 Les Misérables (from a book)
2 France at the beginning of the 19th century
3 a story about the situation of the poor, and the criminal justice system
4 only in outline (it is a very long story)
5 an ex-convict called Valjean, a law enforcement officer called Javert, a bishop, a woman called Fantine, her daughter Cosette and a law student called Marius
6 illegitimate daughter, adopts, false identity, criminal justice system, radical group, ex-convict, mayor, uprising, bishop

b Explain that students are going to retell the story to another student afterwards, and so should make notes in order to help them do so. Play the recording again for students to check their answers and make notes.

4 Put students into pairs with one member from each of the groups. Students retell the stories as best they can. Monitor and make notes on students' language for later feedback.

5 Focus attention on the Useful language box. Students find the phrases in the audio script. In feedback, drill the phrases with the class.

ANSWERS:

Story A: It's told in the first person., The tension builds up., It's a bit ambiguous., It's a very chilling story., You have a strong sense of unease.

Story B: It's set in ... , The story opens as ... , It's extremely long., Parts of it are heartbreaking / very uplifting., It's so moving.

Task (PAGE 23)

Speaking

1a Students decide if they want to work alone or in pairs. Give them plenty of time to choose a story and check the details online.

b Students plan their talks. Go around and help with ideas and vocabulary, writing any new words/phrases on the board.

2 Students work in pairs to practise telling their stories. Explain that this is a 'practice run', so they should take the opportunity to give each other feedback on how they tell the story.

3 With smaller classes, ask students to tell their stories to the class. With larger classes, put students into groups to tell their stories. Monitor and make notes on the students' use of language for later class feedback. When they have finished, ask students which stories they liked best.

Follow up (PAGE 23)

Writing

1   This could be done in class or for homework.

> **Share your task**
>
> Some additional ideas could include:
> - Students draw/create a storyboard, with key events of the story, then film/record themselves describing it.
> - Students work in groups and create a film/book/play review programme, which they film/record. Other students watch/listen to the recording and choose which they'd like to see.
> - Students work in small groups and film/record themselves acting out a scene from the film/book/play.
> - In pairs, students prepare an interview with one of the main characters of the story, which they then act out and film/record, with one of the students taking the role of the character and the other taking the role of an interviewer.
> - Students film/record themselves retelling the story, but with two different endings. Others students watch/listen to the recording and choose which one they like best.

ADDITIONAL PRACTICE

➡ **Workbook:** Writing: *Plot summary*, page 13

World culture (PAGES 24–25)

Luxury superbrands

> **Culture notes**
>
> A luxury superbrand is an extremely popular brand of luxury goods, which is often used as a status symbol or symbol of wealth. Some of the world's main luxury brands include the French fashion houses Louis Vuitton, founded in 1854 and with an annual global turnover of $9.4 billion, Chanel, founded by Coco Chanel in 1909 and with an annual global turnover of $4.4 billion, and Gucci, founded in Florence in 1921 and Italy's biggest selling brand.
>
> Other brands include luxury car maker Rolls Royce, founded in 1906 and with an annual global turnover of $19.77 billion, watchmakers Rolex and luxury jewellery makers Tiffany and Co.
>
> Technology has also been integrated into luxury goods, with Japanese fashion and fragrance designer Issey Miyake integrating technology into his designs, and luxury mobile phone maker Vertu.
>
> The world's biggest market for luxury goods is Japan, though this is expected to be overtaken by China in the near future, which is currently the world's second biggest market. Overall, it is estimated that the world spends just under $3 billion on luxury goods a year.

Find out first (PAGE 24)

1a You could bring/download photos of luxury goods produced by these brands (or their logos) and see how many the students can identify. Find out how much students know about each one, then feed in information from the Culture notes (being careful not to give away the answers to the quiz in exercise 2a). Elicit any other luxury brands students can think of.

b   Students discuss in pairs, then share answers with the class.

2a Check understanding of *turnover* (total value of sales, also called *income* and *revenue*). Students do the quiz in pairs or small groups.

b   If possible, students go online to check their answers, using the search terms in the box. Otherwise students check answers with you.

> **ANSWERS:**
>
> 1 c   2 a   3 a   4 b   5 a   6 a

View (PAGE 24)

See *Teaching tips: Using the video material in the classroom*, page 24.

3a With weaker classes, check understanding of the words in the box first by eliciting examples of things which can be described in this way. Answer the question as a class.

> **POSSIBLE ANSWERS:**
>
> exclusive, high-end, slick

b   ▶ Go through the sentences and elicit students' predictions, then play the DVD for them to check.

> **ANSWERS:**
>
> 1 wouldn't   2 bottom

4   Students attempt to answer the questions from memory, then play the DVD again for them to check, then check in pairs. Check answers with the whole class.

> **ANSWERS:**
>
> 1 a, c   2 a, c   3 b   4 b

5   Students discuss the questions in pairs. In feedback, elicit their ideas and have a brief class discussion.

World view (PAGE 25)

6a ▶ Play the DVD straight through, encouraging students to just listen for whether they approve or disapprove of luxury brands.

b   Students check in pairs then check answers with the class. Elicit any reasons students heard, but don't give any answers yet.

7   Play the DVD again, pausing after each speaker for students to make notes, then check in pairs. Check answers with the class, nominating different students to summarise each speaker's view.

> **ANSWERS:**
>
> **Sophie:** ✓ Luxury brands encourage people to work hard.
>
> **Jurgen:** ✓/✗ They're not good or bad, just a waste of money. He only buys luxury food as it's important to eat well.
>
> **Keith:** ✗ He doesn't trust big brands, as he thinks that they spend a lot of money on marketing at the expense of the quality of the product.
>
> **Luis:** ✓/✗ Luxury brands create innovations which drive the economy, but people who can't afford them end up spending a lot of money on something they don't need.
>
> **Clare:** ✓ Luxury brands aren't essential, but it's nice to treat yourself now and then. She buys a balance of luxury brands and 'value packs'.
>
> **Sayful:** ✗ Luxury brands make people envious of each other, so negative. He only buys luxury brands he can afford.
>
> **Imogen:** ✗ She's not interested in luxury brands and has a friend who chooses a partner according to what trainers he wears, which she doesn't understand.

8   Students discuss in pairs, then discuss as a class.

Find out more 🔊 (PAGE 25)

9a Write the marketing techniques on the board, and elicit students' ideas about what they mean, and any examples they know.

b Students choose a technique and, depending on how big your class is, research it online alone or in pairs.

> **Find out more: Alternative suggestion**
>
> After researching one of the types of advertising, students prepare a short advert or commercial in the style of the marketing technique they've researched, then present it to the class.

Present your research

10 Go through the prompts, eliciting possible endings, and read the Tip with the class. Give students plenty of time to prepare their presentations, and help with vocabulary where necessary. When they are ready, students take turns presenting their findings. Encourage other students to listen and make notes, so that they can ask questions at the end of each presentation.

Students can now do Progress Test 1 on the Teacher's Resource Disc.

Grammar practice (PAGES 118–119)

See *Teaching tips: Using the Grammar and Vocabulary practice sections*, page 25.

Perfect verb forms

ANSWERS:

1
1 A The speaker is interested in whether the person has finished cleaning.
B The speaker is interested in how the person has been spending their time.
2 A The speaker sees 'today' as not finished, i.e. it is afternoon or early evening.
B The speaker sees 'today' as finished, i.e. it is late at night.
3 A Suggests that the visits are recent.
B Suggests 'in my life', not necessarily recently.
4 No significant difference in meaning.

2
1 never **2** recently **3** last week **4** several times
5 a long time **6** for a week

3
Sentence 3 is correct.
1 I've asked **2** I've been sitting **4** we'd just been talking
5 you've worked **6** until he got

4
A
1 heard **2** had left **3** wasn't **4** had happened **5** didn't answer
6 phoned **7** found out **8** 'd gone **9** 'd been stealing ('d stolen is also possible, but 'd been stealing emphasises that the action was repeated) **10** 've known **11** 've ever met **12** have made
B
1 had been
2 arrived
3 had left (left is also possible because the sequence of events is made obvious by after)
4 had been hiding (hid is also possible, but had been hiding emphasises the duration of the activity)
5 hadn't intended
6 'd got (got is also possible because the sequence of events is obvious)
7 (had) decided
8 'd never given up (the Past perfect is preferred here because it is reported speech)

6
1 Having waited ages for a waiter to take my order, I decided to go somewhere else.
2 Amy's told so many lies in the past that nobody will believe her this time. / Nobody will believe Amy this time because she's told so many lies in the past.
3 Having looked at all the applications, we've decided to offer you the job.
4 I've been here lots of times before, so the shop assistant knows me. / The shop assistant knows me because I've been here lots of times before.
5 Having seen the weather forecast, we decided not to play golf.
6 Having never done an operation before, the doctor was quite nervous.

7
1 d, take **2** c, to have disappeared **3** g, to have seen
4 f, have gone **5** h, have enjoyed **6** e, to be
7 b, to have survived **8** a, to sit

8
1 You've been reading that book for ages!
2 I bet Hannah wishes she hadn't bought that games console.
3 It was the second time I'd seen that film.
4 We haven't enjoyed ourselves so much for ages.
5 Having never spoken in public before, Leonie was very nervous.
6 I wouldn't like to have lived in the 18th century.

9
1 *it's been* – unspecified time in the past
2 *I've changed* – happened in the past but relevant to the present
3 *he'd been sitting* – emphasises the duration of the action before a point in the past ('he collapsed')
4 *I've known* – incomplete state
5 *I've come* – happened in the past but relevant to the present
have come – perfect infinitive used after *should*, to emphasise the past
I've been standing – emphasises the duration of the action
6 *had been* – reported speech after 'declared'; the misprint is *hug* instead of *huge*

Vocabulary practice (PAGE 153)
Feelings

ANSWERS:
1
1 ashamed **2** apprehensive **3** mortified
4 under a lot of pressure **5** disgusted **6** overjoyed **7** desperate
8 cross

Idioms with *laugh*, *cry* and *tears*

ANSWERS:
2
1 she's in *rivers* **floods** of tears
2 we'll all be *boring* **bored** to tears
3 Dominique burst *off* **out** laughing
4 but we had the last *tears* **laugh**
5 the audience was close to *cry* **tears**
6 no laughing *thing* **matter**

Other words and phrases

ANSWERS:
3
1 pamper **2** turn people off **3** aspirations **4** fitted
5 heavily regulated **6** setting up **7** backfired **8** set out to

OVERVIEW

PAGES 26–27

Vocabulary and speaking: Money and enterprise

Common European Framework: Students can use a good range of vocabulary for most general topics; can express their ideas and opinions with precision.

PAGES 28–29

Reading and speaking: But are they worth it?

Grammar review: Time and tense

Common European Framework: Students can understand in detail a wide range of complex texts; can hold their own in formal discussion of complex issues, putting forward an articulate and persuasive argument.

PAGES 30–31

Listening: The case of Stella Liebeck

Patterns to notice: Inversion with negative adverbials

Wordspot: *worth*

Common European Framework: Students can identify finer points of detail including implicit attitudes and relationships between speakers; can exploit a range of language to give emphasis.

PAGES 32–33

Task: Decide which project to back

Common European Framework: Students can outline an issue or a problem clearly, speculating about causes or consequences, and weighing advantages and disadvantages of different approaches.

PAGES 34–35

Speaking: Describing quantities

Writing: Summarising statistics

Common European Framework: Students can select an appropriate formulation from a broad range of language to express themselves clearly; can write clear, well-structured reports.

Vocabulary and speaking

(PAGES 26–27)

Money and enterprise

See *Teaching tips: Working with lexis*, page 21.

WARM UP

Do a 'currency quiz'. Put students into teams, and explain you will say some currencies from around the world. Students listen and write the country where the currency is used. When you have finished, check answers and award a point for each correct country. The team with the most points wins. Currencies to read out: 1 Yen (Japan), 2 Real (Brazil), 3 Rupee (India), 4 Ruble (Russia), 5 Riyal (Saudi Arabia), 6 Baht (Thailand).

1a Put students into pairs and focus them on the quiz. Stress that they should guess the meaning of unfamiliar vocabulary, rather than asking you or consulting a dictionary. You could give them a time limit (e.g. three minutes) to add an element of competition.

b 🎧 **3.1** You could stop the recording before playing each answer and have pairs call out their answers, then play that section of the recording and see how many pairs were right. Check the pronunciation of: *worthless* /ˈwɜːθlɪs/, *stingy* /ˈstɪndʒi/, *ransom* /ˈrænsəm/ and *maintenance* /ˈmeɪntənəns/.

ANSWERS:
1 D   2 B   3 A
4 A ✗   B ✓   C ✗   D ✗
5 1 D, 2 C, 3 E, 4 A, 5 B
6 A – a waiter, from a customer
  B – a pensioner, from the government
  C – a child from his/her parent
  D – a kidnapper, from a kidnapping victim's family
  E – a husband/wife from his/her ex-partner
7 A (R)   B (B)   C (R)   D (R)   E (R)   F (B)   G (B)   H (B)   I (B)

Vocabulary and speaking, exercise 1b: Alternative suggestion

Award extra 'bonus' sums of money (e.g. $10 per correct explanation) to any pair who can explain why other options in the question are wrong.

2a Give students a few minutes to go through the questions individually, then put them into pairs to compare and help each other with answers they were unsure of.

b Give students a few minutes to think of other questions. Go around and help with ideas where necessary. When they are ready, put students into groups to ask and answer the questions.

3 Direct students to the quiz, and give them time to complete the word web individually or in pairs.

POSSIBLE ANSWERS:
1 businesses going bust, economic expansion, government spending cuts, high property prices, high salaries, high share prices, high unemployment, an increase in GDP, a large government deficit
2 be in the black, be in the red, break even, go bankrupt, make a large profit
3 an advance, alimony/maintenance, a bribe, a deposit, a fee, a pension, pocket money, a ransom, a tip
4 a bribe
5 flashy, penny-pinching, stingy, tight
6 priceless, pricey, worthless
7 alimony/maintenance, a pension, a tip
8 broke, flashy, hard-up, loaded, skint

4a Put students into groups to discuss the sayings. With weaker classes, you may want to check understanding of the phrases as a class.

b While students are thinking of their reasons, go around and help where necessary. Students then either work in the same groups or walk around the room speaking to other students as a mingle activity. Monitor and note down examples of good language use and/or errors for feedback and correction later.

ADDITIONAL PRACTICE

➡ **Resource bank:** Activity 3C *Priceless* (Money and enterprise)

Vocabulary practice: Exercise 1

Workbook: Vocabulary: *Money and enterprise*, page 14

Reading and speaking (PAGES 28–29)

But are they worth it?

1 Write on the board: *actor, teacher, nurse, TV presenter, dentist, construction worker*. Ask students which of these jobs pay well and which pay badly in their country/ies. Students then think of two more examples of professions which are overpaid and underpaid in pairs. When they are ready, nominate students to share their ideas with the class and have a brief class discussion.

2 Students read the first two paragraphs then discuss the question in pairs. Elicit their ideas in feedback.

3 Read the examples with the class. Students read the article and complete the arguments alone then check in pairs. Ask early finishers to come and write their answers on the board then ask if the class agrees.

4 Students read the article again then answer the questions in pairs, before checking answers with the whole class.

5 Refer students back to the word web on page 27 before they find words/phrases in the article. In feedback, write the words on the board and check understanding.

6 Briefly outline what each option involves, then ask the students to vote for which option they prefer via a show of hands. With larger classes, the Discussion is probably a better option as more students will have the chance to participate. Either way, make notes on students' language use while they are speaking for later feedback with the class.

ADDITIONAL PRACTICE
Workbook: Listen and read: *Mobile affluenza clinics*, pages 14–15

Grammar review (PAGE 29)

Time and tense

See *Teaching tips: Using a discovery approach to grammar*, page 20.

1a Focus attention on the photo and elicit who it is (Cristiano Ronaldo). Ask students if footballers are paid a lot of money in their country/ies. Students read the article and name the forms of the verbs. Check answers with the whole class.

b Go through the example with the class. While students are completing the table, copy it onto the board. In feedback, invite students to come to the board to complete the first column.

2a Go through the example with the class. Students complete the second column of the table alone then check in pairs. In feedback, invite students to the board to complete the second column.

b Students discuss in pairs. Check answers with the whole class, and go through the ideas in the language notes.

Notes on time and tense

In English, time and tense are different things. Time is a universal concept, which refers to past, present, future and general time. Tense is a grammatical concept and describes how we change the structure of a verb. A more realistic way to describe past and present tenses is in terms of distance. 'Present' tenses show that things are 'close' to us, whereas 'past' tenses show that things are 'distant' to us. Our choice of tense in this respect depends on one (or more) of three things: *time*, *reality* and *formality*. In order to illustrate this, you could draw the following diagram on the board:

Remote ◄		► Close
When I was a child, I walked to school.	**Time**	I go to work by bus.
I wish I was/were rich.	**Reality**	I'm not rich.
Could you possibly open the window, please?	**Formality**	Can you open the window?

You may want to ask students to read Language summary 3 on pages 120–121 for a more detailed explanation of time and tense.

3 Put students into pairs, then direct them to the relevant pages and check they understand what to do. As they are discussing the sentences, monitor and help where necessary. Encourage them to refer to the chart you drew on the board in exercise 2b when describing the time references. When they have finished, check answers with the class.

ADDITIONAL PRACTICE
➡ **Resource bank:** Activity 3A *Where's it from?* (Time and tense)
Grammar practice: Exercises 1–9
Workbook: Grammar: *Time and tense*, pages 16–17

Listening (PAGES 30–31)
The case of Stella Liebeck

1a Focus students on the pictures and give them a minute or two to find illustrations of the words in the box. Check the pronunciation of: *damages* /ˈdæmɪdʒɪz/, *scalding* /ˈskɔːldɪŋ/, *to sue* /suː/ and *jury* /ˈdʒʊəri/.

ANSWERS:
A drop someone off   B damages   F lid, tug   G jury, sue
H horrified, scalding

b 🎧 **3.2** Students could work in pairs and predict a possible order for the pictures, before they listen. Once students have checked their answers, they could practise retelling the story in their own words, using the pictures as prompts.

ANSWERS:
1 A   2 D   3 F   4 H   5 C   6 E   7 G   8 B

Listening, exercise 1b: Additional activity
If you want to check that students have understood some of the facts in the story, give them the following questions and play the recording again:
How old was Stella Liebeck? (79)
Who was driving the car at the burger restaurant? (her grandson, Chris)
Why did the coffee spill on her lap? (Because she had the cup between her knees and tried to pull the lid off.)
How long was she in hospital? (eight days)
How much were her medical expenses and how much did the company offer her? (Her expenses were about $2,000. The company offered her $800.)
How much did she eventually receive in compensation? ($640,000)

2a 🎧 **3.3** Students make notes while they listen to the people arguing.

ANSWERS:
1 in favour of Stella:
– the coffee is hotter than normal coffee: 180–190 degrees Fahrenheit (normal coffee is only 135–140 degrees Fahrenheit)
– there had previously been about 700 cases of people being burnt by scalding coffee
– the fast-food chain makes $1.3 million a day from selling coffee
2 in favour of the company:
– Stella refused to accept it was her fault
– people know coffee is hot, it's their fault if they spill it
– it leads to more and more ridiculous claims

b Discuss this question as a class.

3 Put students into small groups to discuss their opinions. Possible disadvantages of a 'compensation culture' might include:
– companies will begin to cover themselves against any possible claims, so it will be more difficult to win compensation when it is really deserved
– retail companies might increase their prices, to cover the money they pay out in compensation
– it could lead to people being dishonest, and inventing stories just to win compensation

PATTERNS TO NOTICE
Inversion with negative adverbials
1 🎧 **3.4** Give students a minute or two to try to put the words in order. If they find it difficult, give them the first word in each case, i.e.: 1 Only, 2 Not once, 3 No way. Play the recording for students to check, then write the correct sentences on the board. Go through the form and use of these examples before continuing.

ANSWERS:
1 Only then did Stella consult a lawyer.
2 Not once did she admit that it was her fault.
3 No way should she have been given all that money.

• Get students to tell you how these sentences would be worded without the adverbials and write the answers on the board, i.e. 1 She didn't consult a lawyer before then.; 2 She never admitted / did not once admit that it was her fault.; 3 She should definitely not have been given all that money.
• Ask students what difference the adverbials make, i.e. they add emphasis, and point out that *Only then* and *Not once* are used in formal language, whereas *No way* is informal.
• Establish what happens to the word order after the adverbials, i.e. the subject and verb are inverted and the auxiliary *do* is used if necessary, as in a question form. Point out that because the adverbials are negative in meaning, the verb after them changes to the positive, e.g.
She did not once admit … → Not once did she admit …

2 & 3 Focus students on the information in the box and give them a few minutes to read through the examples. Answer any questions they have.

Potential problem with inversions
Students often have problems remembering the correct word order in inversions with negative adverbials. It can help to draw a similarity between question forms and the order of words after the negative adverbial.

4 Students work individually and compare answers in pairs.

ANSWERS:
1 No longer does our country need to rely on foreign investment.
2 Under no circumstances should you borrow money without checking the interest rates.
3 Only now are we seeing the benefits of the government's policies.
4 Rarely has a change of government had such a dramatic effect on the economic outlook.
5 Frederick looked for his wallet to pay. Only then did he realise he had left all his money at home.
6 On no account should you reveal the details of your bank account over the telephone.
7 Never before has this country witnessed such a serious financial crisis.
8 Seldom does a politician admit publicly that he has made a mistake.
9 Not only did George have to pay a large fine, but he also had to spend some time in prison.

5a 🎧 **3.5** Students listen and match the speakers to the situations. Check answers with the class.

ANSWERS:
1 d   2 b   3 a   4 e   5 c

b Play the recording again for students to identify the adverbial used by each speaker.

ANSWERS:
1 Not only   2 Never before   3 Only now   4 No way
5 Under no circumstances

6a Students write sentences about their own ideas, using the sentences in exercise 5a as examples. Monitor and check students are forming the sentences correctly.

b Students compare their sentences in pairs. You could ask them to read out their sentences for their partner to guess which of the situations in exercise 5a it describes.

ADDITIONAL PRACTICE
➡ **Resource bank:** Activity 3B *Under no circumstances ...* (Inversion with negative adverbials)
Workbook: Grammar: *Inversion with negative adverbials*, page 17

Wordspot (PAGE 31)
worth

See *Teaching tips: Working with lexis*, page 21.

1a Explain that students need to match the explanations to only six of the words/phrases. Students work alone then check in pairs, before checking answers with the whole class.

ANSWERS:
a 1   b 6   c 4   d 10   e 12   f 5

b Students think of definitions in pairs. When they are ready, students share their definitions with the class.

POSSIBLE ANSWERS:
2 has no value, importance or use
3 interesting or useful
7 interesting or useful
8 useful for you to spend time doing it
9 the equivalent value of five pounds
11 enough (food) for two days

> **Wordspot, exercise 1b: Alternative suggestion**
> Students work alone to write a definition for each of the six words/phrases, checking the meanings in monolingual dictionaries or on their mobile phones. When they are ready, put students into pairs to test each other. One student reads out their definition for their partner to guess the word/phrase.

2 Go through the examples with the class, then students complete the rest of the word web alone. Check answers with the class.

ANSWERS:
1 worth a fortune
2 worth keeping, well worth the effort, worth a quick look, be worth your while
3 five pounds' worth, two days' worth
4 for what it's worth, prove your worth
5 worthless, worthwhile, worthy

3a 🎧 **3.6** Before students listen, explain that they need to write short answers and write them in random order. Play the recording, pausing after each instruction for students to write their answers.

b Students discuss their answers in pairs. In feedback, nominate students to share any interesting information they found out about their partner.

ADDITIONAL PRACTICE
➡ **Resource bank:** Activity 3D *For what it's worth* (*worth*)
Vocabulary practice: Exercise 2
Workbook: Wordspot: *worth*, page 18

Task (PAGES 32–33)
Decide which project to back

See *Teaching tips: Making tasks work*, page 23.

WARM UP
Explain that you are going to give students $5,000 to start their own project or create their own invention. Give students a few minutes to think about what they would do individually, then put students into small groups to share their ideas. When they have finished, ask groups to choose the best idea to share with the class.

Preparation (PAGES 32–33)
Reading and vocabulary

1 Give students one minute to read the introduction then answer the question in pairs. Check answers with the class.

ANSWERS:
It aims to provide a platform for people to attract investment. Supporters can pledge any amount from $20 to $500.

2 Elicit/Check: *props* (objects which actors use on stage), *planning permission* (permission from the local government to build something), *showcase talents* (demonstrate what you can do) and *premises* (property). Students read about the five projects and make notes. In feedback, nominate different students to summarise each project for the class.

3 Students check the meaning of the words in bold, and ask you about any they're not sure of. When they are ready, students discuss the questions in pairs.

ANSWERS:
entrepreneurial: willing to take risks in business
favourable publicity: positive coverage in the media
keep up with demand: be able to produce as many as people want
self-funded: pays for itself
marketing costs: the amount of money you spend on promoting your product or service
collaborative: characterised by people working together
environmentally friendly: kind to the environment, doesn't cause pollution
non-profit-making: doesn't aim to make money
community-based: takes place in the local area
innovative: original and new, something which hasn't been done before
quirky: strange or unusual in a positive way
commercially successful: popular and therefore able to make a profit

4 Elicit some benefits of the first project as an example, e.g. *material: new costumes, props, etc.; altruistic: educational*. Students discuss the benefits of the other projects in pairs.

Task (PAGES 32–33)

Speaking

1 Refer students to the Useful language box, section a. Students work alone to decide on their priorities for investment, using the questions as guidelines.

2 Explain that students can allocate different amounts of money to the projects (i.e. they don't have to invest it all in one project), and must try to agree as a group on exactly how the money will be spent. Go through the phrases in the Useful language box, section b. As they discuss the investment, go around and make notes on students' language use for later class feedback.

Task, Speaking: Additional activity

Students listen to and analyse a 'model' of the task: make a recording of yourself and one or two other people (e.g. teachers in the school) discussing the same five cases and deciding on the amounts of sponsorship. Incorporate some of the phrases from the Useful language box where possible. Students listen and compare your conclusions with theirs, then focus on the language you used (e.g. by ticking off phrases from the Useful language box). If you have time to make a transcript of the recording, they can read through this and find examples of useful phrases.

---

3 Go through the phrases in the Useful language box, section c and give students a few minutes to decide how they are going to present their decisions. Groups take it in turn to present their decisions to the class.

Share your task

Some additional ideas could include:

- Students work in five groups, with each group representing one of the projects on pages 32–33. Each student films/records themselves giving a presentation/pitch for the project. Other students then watch/listen to the pitches and choose the best one.
- Students invent their own project for the website, then film/record themselves giving a presentation/pitch for their idea. Other students watch/listen to the recordings and choose one they'd like to invest in.
- Students record 'vox pop' style three-minute interviews with people who have benefitted from some of the projects.
- Students record interviews with group members from the task, explaining why they allocated the money the way they did.

Language live (PAGES 34–35)

Speaking (PAGE 34)

Describing quantities

WARM UP

Write the following on the board:

the population of your country, the number of countries in the world, how many cups of coffee you've had this month, how much you've spent on clothes in the past year, the GDP of your country, the number of students in your school

Students discuss the numbers in pairs. When they are ready, ask students to share their ideas with the class. They don't need to guess correctly, but pay attention to how they give approximate values at this stage. If they want to, they can go online to find out the larger numbers.

---

1 You could start by discussing why people might want to use a phrase from the box rather than be precise, i.e. to add emphasis, exaggerate the quantity or use the appropriate tone for spoken English. Students work individually or in pairs to replace the bold quantities in the sentences with phrases from the box.

ANSWERS:
1 a small percentage   2 a small quantity   3 A vast number of
4 a dash   5 an enormous portion   6 the overwhelming majority
7 a huge sum of money   8 a pinch   9 a great deal of time
10 dozens of   11 a handful   12 a while

2 You could do the first example with the class – possible phrases depending on where students are from: *the overwhelming majority of; a small percentage of; a handful of; dozens of; a vast number of*. When students have completed all the sentences, they could compare with a partner or walk around the class comparing with others.

Writing (PAGES 34–35)

Summarising statistics

1 Students discuss the question in pairs. When they are ready, ask them to read the article quickly, ignoring the gaps, to find any other ideas. In feedback, elicit their ideas and write them on the board.

ANSWERS:
mobile phones, digital music

2a Make sure students understand that there is one extra word/phrase in each set. Students work alone then check in pairs, before checking answers with the whole class.

ANSWERS:
1 steadily   2 dramatically   3 increase/rise   4 Overall
5 gone up   6 increase/rise   7 By far   8 triple   9 Much less
10 significantly   11 respectively   12 In contrast   13 sharply
14 slightly

b Go through the examples with the class, then students find further examples. In feedback, write the phrases on the board.

POSSIBLE ANSWERS:
risen steadily, risen dramatically, the biggest increase, twelvefold increase/rise, increased significantly, fallen sharply, dropped slightly

3 Discuss this question with the whole class.

4a Refer students back to exercise 2 to notice how the words/phrases are used. Students work alone then check in pairs. Check answers with the whole class.

ANSWERS:
1 much less   2 significantly/sharply/dramatically   3 respectively
4 Overall   5 In contrast   6 slightly   7 By far   8 increase/rise
9 doubled, tripled

b Students work in pairs. When they have finished, nominate students to read out their sentences to the class.

5 Students guess the missing numbers in pairs. Make sure they don't look at the article yet.

6 Students complete the article. Check answers with the class before referring them back to the table in exercise 5 to check their answers. Find out how many students guessed correctly.

ANSWERS:
1 than 2 as 3 a 4 of 5 as 6 on 7 a 8 a 9 than
(Possible answers)

	Single men	Single women
electronics	€15	€10
personal care	€21	€41
clothing	€44	€66
pets	€16	€23.5
food shopping	€133	€133.5
going out	€15	€14
eating out	€102	€80

7a Give students a few minutes to study the bar chart, then discuss the question as a class.

b Refer back to the two articles for students to use as models, and encourage them to use the vocabulary from exercise 2. When students have written their articles, ask them to swap with a partner to read.

ADDITIONAL PRACTICE

➡ **Workbook:** Language live: *Describing quantities*, page 18; Writing: *Summarising statistics*, page 18

Grammar practice (PAGES 122–123)

See *Teaching tips: Using the Grammar and Vocabulary practice sections*, page 25.

Time and tense

ANSWERS:
1
2 Footballer scores hat trick but team beaten.
3 President hints at changes in privacy laws.
4 Blues singer Leroy Morganfield collapses on stage at Newfield Stadium.
5 TV company fined after three-year court case.
6 Mother and daughter fall from balcony but both OK.
2
1 leaves 2 catches 3 arrives 4 is 5 meets 6 orders 7 brings 8 has 9 shouts 10 replies 11 finds 12 decides 13 meet 14 has 15 change
3
1 I declare – an important person opening a new museum
2 Dyson passes, he shoots – a football commentator
3 I chop – a TV chef
4 I swear – a witness in court
5 we're going – a tour guide
6 I name – an important person launching a new ship
7 I suggest – a police officer questioning a suspect
8 The minister's coming, are jostling – a news reporter
4
1 e 2 c 3 f 4 a 5 b 6 h 7 d 8 g
5
1 what, f 2 by the time, c 3 before, g 4 while, e 5 whether, b 6 who, h 7 until, a 8 if, d

6
1 Jamie would sooner we met at his house.
2 If I was/were in your position, I'd be careful.
3 I wondered if I could possibly ask you a huge favour.
4 It's time Abi's parents let her go on holiday with her friends.
5 I wish I didn't have to work until 8:00 this evening.
6 If they were to offer me the job, I'd be over the moon.
7 I'd rather you didn't mention this to anyone.
7
(Possible answers)
1 didn't understand, would you communicate
2 could live, would you live
3 take, would you go
4 could go, would you go
5 could meet, would you meet
8
1 If it hadn't been for her, I'd never have done it.
2 I wouldn't have missed that for anything!
3 So would you do it again?
4 I wish I'd started training earlier.
5 I would have been better prepared.
6 There was one more thing I wanted to ask you …
7 It's time I got to the studio …
9
1 both sound natural
2 *hasn't got*
3 both are correct, but *don't* sounds more natural, because the fact is still important now
4 *was telling*
5 *wanted*
6 both sound natural, both sound natural

Vocabulary practice (PAGE 154)
Money and enterprise

ANSWERS:
1
1 loaded 2 broke even 3 pricey 4 ransom 5 high unemployment 6 tip 7 flashy

worth

ANSWERS:
2
1 a 2 b 3 b 4 a 5 b 6 a

Other words and phrases

ANSWERS:
3
1 entrepreneurial 2 got off to a flying 3 non-profit-making 4 quirky 5 favourable publicity 6 collaborative

04 SELF-HELP

OVERVIEW

PAGES 36–37

Vocabulary and speaking: Self-improvement

Pronunciation: Word stress

Common European Framework: Students can summarise information from different sources; can weigh advantages and disadvantages of different approaches to solving problems.

PAGES 38–39

Listening and vocabulary: Fitness

Patterns to notice: Patterns with comparatives and superlatives

Wordspot: Body idioms

Common European Framework: Students can follow discussions with relative ease; have a good command of idiomatic expressions.

PAGES 40–41

Reading: Dear Me ...

Grammar review: Adjectives

Common European Framework: Students can understand any correspondence; can express themselves with clarity and precision in personal correspondence, use language flexibly and effectively including emotional, allusive and joking usage.

PAGES 42–43

Task: Decide who wins the award

Common European Framework: Students can outline an issue or a problem clearly, speculating about causes or consequences, and weighing advantages and disadvantages of different approaches.

PAGES 44–45

World culture: Three minutes of exercise

Common European Framework: Students can follow lectures, discussions and debates with relative ease; can give a clear, detailed description of how to carry out a procedure.

Vocabulary and speaking

(PAGES 36–37)

Self-improvement

See *Teaching tips: Working with lexis*, page 21.

WARM UP

Write the following phrases on the board:

do exercise, eat junk food, do nothing, watch TV, drive somewhere within walking distance, do something just for yourself

Students ask each other how often they do each of the things in pairs. In feedback, ask students to tell you how healthy they think their partner is.

1a Give students a few minutes to read the list and check they understand the activities. Encourage them to use their mobile phone to look up words they're not sure of, and answer any questions they have about the vocabulary.

b Put students into groups to discuss the questions. Follow up by asking students if they have tried or do any of these activities.

2a Go through the examples with the class, then students work in pairs to do the rest. In feedback, check understanding of the phrases, especially: *broadens your horizons* (gives you a wider perspective on life), *gives you a sense of perspective* (helps you see things as they really are), *keep it up* (maintain), *uneasy* (uncomfortable) and *tests your endurance* (improves your stamina).

ANSWERS:

3 B	4 B	5 B	6 B	7 D	8 B	9 B	10 D	11 D
12 B	13 D	14 B	15 D	16 B	17 D	18 B	19 D
20 B

b Students discuss the question in pairs. In feedback, nominate students to share their ideas with the class, and find out if other students agree.

3a 🎧 **4.1** Play the recording, pausing after each word for students to practise saying it. Pay attention to how students are pronouncing the following words, and drill if necessary: *acupuncture* /ˈækjʊpʌŋktʃə/, *discipline* /ˈdɪsɪplɪn/, *spirituality* /spɪrɪtʃuˈwælɪti/ and *laser* /ˈleɪzə/.

b Students practise saying the words on their own. Go around and help where necessary.

4a Students read the descriptions and note their ideas alone.

b Put students into groups to compare their ideas. When they have finished, nominate one student from each group to present their ideas and reasons to the class.

5 Give students a few minutes to decide which activities they would/wouldn't like to try and why on their own. When they are ready, rearrange students into new groups to discuss their ideas.

ADDITIONAL PRACTICE

Resource bank: Activity 4C *Good for your health* (Self-improvement and fitness)

Vocabulary practice: Exercise 1

Workbook: Vocabulary: *Self-improvement*, page 19; Pronunciation: *Schwa*, page 19

Listening and vocabulary

(PAGES 38–39)

Fitness

WARM UP

Put students into pairs, and give them one minute to brainstorm different ways of getting fit. After one minute, stop them and elicit their ideas, then write them on the board. Students can refer back to these when discussing the questions in exercise 1.

1 Introduce the topic by telling the class about what you do to keep fit (or if you've ever tried to get really fit). Students discuss the questions in groups.

2a Focus attention on the photos, and elicit how the people are getting fit. Ask students if they do / have ever done these things.

ANSWERS:

from left to right: working out in the gym / doing weights; running in a race/marathon; running / using an app to train

b 🎧 **4.2** Go through the words/phrases in bold with the class, giving explanations where necessary. Play the recording for students to listen and mark the phrases. Students check in pairs then check answers with the whole class.

ANSWERS:

2 T	3 N	4 H	5 T	6 N	7 T	8 T	9 N	10 H

3 Students discuss the questions in pairs, then listen again and check their answers. Check answers with the class.

ANSWERS:
1 Hannah: her personal trainer; the exercises are varied
Ted: his phone app
Nicola: raising money for charity
2 Students' own answers
3 Hannah: ankle-strengthening exercises
Ted: calculating his metabolic rate; how many calories he needs to eat or lose; getting reminders on his phone to go to the gym; calculating how far he has run or walked; getting nutritional information on his phone
Nicola: running five times a week; running with another person to keep motivated

4 Students discuss the questions in small groups.

PATTERNS TO NOTICE

Patterns with comparatives and superlatives
1 🎧 **4.3** Ask students for the correct way to complete each sentence and write them on the board. As you do so, ask them what the pattern is.

ANSWERS:
1 best ('*The* (superlative) *thing about* …')
2 The more, the more ('*The* (comparative) subject + verb, *the* (comparative) subject + verb.')
3 worse ('*There is nothing* (comparative) *than* …')

2 Go through the sentences with the class and ask them what the pattern is for each one. You could also give them practice in manipulating the patterns by providing different prompts, e.g.
  • '(noun) *is one of the* (superlative) *ways of* …'
    Prompt: *Doing yoga* …
  • '*The* (comparative) subject + verb, *the* (comparative) subject + verb.'
    Prompt: *The healthier you are,* …
  • '*What could be more* (adjective) *than* …'
    Prompt: *What could be more challenging than* …
  • '(noun) *is among the* (superlative) …'
    Prompt: *Swimming* …

> **Potential problems with comparatives and superlatives**
> Watch out for the following slips, and correct them appropriately:
>   • using *then* instead of *than*
>   • using *the* + comparative instead of *the* + superlative
>   • using (noun) *is one of the* (superlative) + <u>singular</u> instead of <u>plural</u>, e.g. *It's one of the tallest building*.

5a Focus attention on the forum entries. Students complete alone then check in pairs, before checking answers with the whole class.

ANSWERS:
1 the   **2** nothing   **3** thing   **4** among   **5** One   **6** could
7 more   **8** best

b Students discuss in pairs. In feedback, nominate students to share their ideas with the class.

6 Encourage students to use structures from the Patterns to notice box. As they are writing, go around and help with vocabulary where necessary, writing any new words/phrases on the board. When they have finished, ask students to swap tips with other students to read.

ADDITIONAL PRACTICE

➡ **Resource bank:** Activity 4B *Comparison race* (Patterns with comparatives and superlatives)

Workbook: Vocabulary: *Fitness*, page 20; Grammar: *Patterns with comparatives and superlatives*, page 20

Wordspot (PAGE 39)
Body idioms

See *Teaching tips: Working with lexis*, page 21.

1a Stronger students may already have one or two 'favourite' idioms using parts of the body. If so, you could start with a brief discussion to allow them to tell the class. Students complete the idioms alone then check in pairs, before checking answers with the whole class. Be prepared to give further examples where necessary.

ANSWERS:
2 face   **3** hair   **4** eye   **5** nose   **6** mouth   **7** neck   **8** head
9 heart   **10** stomach   **11** hands   **12** thumbs   **13** leg   **14** foot

b Focus attention on the cartoons, and answer the question as a class.

ANSWERS:
left: to have butterflies in your stomach
right: to pull someone's leg

> **Wordspot, exercise 1b: Additional activity**
> Students choose one of the other idioms in exercise 1a and draw a picture to illustrate both the words and the idiom, e.g. a person covered in fingers and thumbs, dropping a plate. They then take it in turns to show their pictures to the class for other students to guess the idiom. You could allocate idioms to students to ensure that they don't all choose the same one.

2 Students study the idioms alone then answer the questions in pairs. Elicit their ideas during feedback.

ANSWERS:
food and drink: turn your nose up at something, mouth-watering
worry, sadness or nerves: be a shoulder to cry on, heart-rending, have butterflies in your stomach
embarrassing situations: turn a blind eye to something, all fingers and thumbs, put your foot in it
humour: keep a straight face, pull someone's leg
stressful situations: hair-raising, up to your neck in it, get your head round something
sport: win hands down

3 Put students into pairs and direct them to the appropriate pages. Give them time to read their questions before they start asking and answering.

ADDITIONAL PRACTICE

➡ **Resource bank:** Activity 4D *Body parts* (Body idioms)
Vocabulary practice: Exercise 2
Workbook: Wordspot: *Body idioms*, page 20

Reading (PAGES 40–41)

Dear Me …

WARM UP

Show the class a photo of yourself when you were a teenager (or when you were significantly younger), and tell students about how you were different then compared to now.

1a Go through the example with the class. Students discuss the question in pairs.

b Give the class one or two examples of advice you would give yourself as an example first. Students discuss the questions in pairs. In feedback, nominate students to share their ideas with the class, and find out if anyone had similar answers.

2a Explain that the letters are to young people from their future selves. Students read the letters then guess the jobs in pairs. Check answers with the class.

> **POSSIBLE ANSWERS:**
> **Ria:** a clothes designer
> **Adrian:** a vet
> **Jonah:** a business manager
> **Jiao:** an actor/dancer

b Discuss this question as a class, writing students' ideas on the board.

> **POSSIBLE ANSWERS:**
> **Ria:** was independent and trusting, quarrelled with her mum and had a short temper
> **Adrian:** was serious and sensitive, and wrote bad poetry
> **Jonah:** was entrepreneurial and hard-working
> **Jiao:** was artistic and law-abiding

3 Students work alone then check in pairs. Check answers with the class.

> **ANSWERS:**
> **1** Ria – 'count to ten before you react'
> **2** Jiao – 'Sweet Jiao, it will get better.'
> **3** Jonah – 'Buy low, sell high. That's all you need to know to be a businessman.'
> **4** Jiao – 'You feel as though all you are doing is helping your parents and studying.'
> **5** Adrian – 'Lighten up!'
> **6** Jonah – 'Try to make everyone who works for you feel important.'
> **7** Ria – 'everything that is happening is just part of a much bigger picture and that somehow it will all make sense in the end'
> **8** Ria – 'The person that you hold dearest in life will be taken away from you.'
> **9** Adrian – 'the truth is that you're incredibly lucky to be born in the time and place that you are'
> **10** Jiao – 'There will still be rules, but you'll know when to break them.'
> **11** Adrian – 'but it isn't much good and your future is not in this field'

4 Students discuss the questions in pairs. In feedback, elicit students' ideas and have a brief class discussion.

5a Encourage students to use the context and surrounding words to check the meanings. In feedback, be prepared to give further explanations/examples where necessary.

b Give students a few minutes to choose their phrases, then compare ideas in pairs. Elicit ideas from one or two students in feedback.

6 While students are writing their letters, go around and help with ideas and vocabulary where necessary. When they have finished, students swap letters with another student to read.

> **Reading, exercise 6: Alternative suggestion**
> Ask students to write their letters on a separate piece of paper, and not to include their names on the letter. When they have finished, collect in all the letters, shuffle them, and redistribute to students, making sure each student has somebody else's letter. Give them a few minutes to read the letter and guess who wrote it. Students then walk around the class asking students about their letters until they find who wrote them.

ADDITIONAL PRACTICE

➡ **Workbook:** Listen and read: *Staying young*, page 21

Grammar review (PAGE 41)

Adjectives

See *Teaching tips: Using a discovery approach to grammar*, page 20.

1 Students do the quiz alone, then work in pairs to check answers. Check answers with the class, going through the language notes below.

> **ANSWERS AND LANGUAGE NOTES:**
> **1 a** You shouldn't feel selfish if you do things for yourself sometimes.
> **b** Worry less about your personal appearance and you'll have a great life.
> **c** Don't get upset if you don't always hear people say positive things about you.
> **d** Don't always be rational – it's important to listen to your inner voice.
> **2 a** well-known, easy-going **b** 50-year-old **c** out
> Possible bonus points: *let down, made-up*
> Note that although most compound adjectives are hyphenated, some of the compounds derived from phrasal verbs are not. They often do not have a hyphen when they come after a verb, whereas they do before a noun, e.g. *I'm feeling stressed out, a made-up story*
> **3 a** believable **b** dramatic **c** cheerful
> Possible bonus points: *enjoyable, dependable, domestic, academic, useful, hopeful*
> **4 a** over-confident **b** dishonest
> Possible bonus points: *anti- (= against, e.g. anti-war), mal- (= badly, e.g. maltreated), post- (= after, e.g. post-match chat), pre- (= before, e.g. Pre-Columbian era), under- (= not enough, e.g. underpaid)*
> **5 a** completely **b** pretty **c** a bit
> Possible bonus points: *rather, quite, fairly, slightly*
> For more possible bonus points, refer to the Language summary on pages 124–125

> **Grammar review, exercise 1: Alternative suggestions**
> To add a competitive element:
> **a** put students into teams and give them a time limit. When the time is up, the team who has written the most correct answers wins. Or explain that the first team to finish the quiz will get five extra bonus points, which will be added to their final score.
> **b** copy the quiz questions onto a PowerPoint presentation, then you can reveal one section at a time. Students in pairs or teams race to complete the section, and the first to do so are given two extra bonus points. These are then added to their final score.

You may want to ask students to read Language summary 4 on pages 124–125 for a more detailed explanation of adjectives and adverbs.

ADDITIONAL PRACTICE

➡ **Resource bank:** Activity 4A *Right or wrong?* (Adjectives)
Grammar practice: Exercises 1–9
Workbook: Grammar: *Adjectives*, pages 22–23

Task (PAGES 42–43)

Decide who wins the award

See *Teaching tips: Making tasks work*, page 23.

WARM UP

Ask students to describe someone they admire in pairs. It could be a friend, family member or somebody famous. Ask them to describe what the person does/did and why they admire them.

Preparation (PAGES 42–43)

Listening

1a Focus students on the short text under 'Human Spirit' and ask them for one or two ideas of courageous things that people do, e.g. rescuing someone in a dangerous situation. If there are or have recently been any human interest stories like this in the news, you could remind students of them.

> **ANSWER:**
>
> People who have shown great mental, physical or moral courage.

b Focus attention on the photos and notes. Check understanding of the words/phrases where necessary. Students discuss what the people might have done in groups. Elicit their ideas but don't give any answers yet.

2a 🎧 **4.4** Elicit/Check: *assailant* (someone who attacks another person). Play the recording for students to check their answers to exercise 1b.

> **ANSWERS:**
>
> **A** Camila Batmanghelidjh opened a drop-in centre for under-privileged children when they were not at school. She decided to recruit ex-gangsters and drug dealers as careworkers in her charity for underprivileged children. She believes that no child is born a criminal.
> **B** Jack Slater helped security guards who were being attacked in a shopping mall. Only he helped.
> **C** Lucy Gale helped two drivers who were stuck on a railway line and managed to drive the two cars off the line. She wanted to prevent a serious rail accident.
> **D** Om Prakash had serious burn injuries on his body after pulling eight of his friends out of a burning van. He didn't think about his own safety.
> **E** Martine Wright lost her legs in a bomb attack. However, she taught herself to walk again and began playing wheelchair tennis and sitting volleyball. She then went on to play at the Paralympic Games. She is determined to grab every opportunity that comes her way.

b Students discuss the questions in pairs. Play the recording again if necessary, then nominate a different student to summarise each story for the class.

Task (PAGES 42–43)

Speaking

1a Go through the phrases in the Useful language box, section a, and check understanding by eliciting possible endings. While students are thinking about the candidates, go around helping with vocabulary as necessary, and make sure that students have a clear idea about how each candidate showed courage, e.g. Camila Batmanghelidjh showed moral courage, Jack Slater showed mental (and physical) courage, etc.

b Encourage students to use phrases from the Useful language box while noting their reasons for their order.

2a–b While students are discussing and deciding on a winner and runner-up, monitor the discussions and note down examples of good language use and/or errors for correction later.

3 Suggest that students make a few notes while listening to each other's speeches. Afterwards, students can briefly discuss particularly good arguments, anyone who changed their mind, etc. This would be a good opportunity to give feedback on students' use of language.

> **Task: Alternative suggestion**
>
> If you want to make this more topical for your students, and you have enough time to spread the Preparation and Task sections over two lessons, give students time between the two lessons to research (e.g. on the internet) a human interest story of courage that has recently been in the news and/or is relevant to their country. You could still do the Preparation section with the five stories given, so that students have an idea of what type of story to look for. Each student then brings notes on the story they have found to the next lesson, and students present their stories to each other in small groups. You can then work through stages 1–3 of the Task using the students' stories. You may want to research and prepare notes on one or two extra stories yourself for students who were unable to find anything.

Follow up (PAGE 43)

Writing

1 Students can make some notes for this and write a first draft in class. Then they can edit their work and write a second draft for homework. Suggest that they also think of a catchy three or four-word headline for the article. Suggested order for the article:
first paragraph: introduce the ceremony, referring to the TV programme; describe the venue where the ceremony is taking place, the famous people who are there, the atmosphere
second paragraph: tell the readers in some detail about the winner and what they achieved; describe the winner's reaction when presented with the award, with some quotes from their speech; refer to the runner-up, then briefly to the other finalists
third paragraph: refer back to the winner and give an opinion about how much they deserved the award; conclude the article, perhaps with some kind of 'moral' about what we can all learn from this

> **Share your task**
>
> Some additional ideas could include:
> - Students imagine they are one of the people on pages 42–43 who has won the award. They prepare, then film/record themselves giving an acceptance speech.
> - Students work in pairs and prepare an interview with one of the people, then film/record it, with one student taking the role of the individual, and the other the interviewer.
> - Students think of someone else they know who they would like to give the award to, then film/record themselves giving a short description of who it is and why. Other students watch/listen to the recording and decide who wins the award.

ADDITIONAL PRACTICE

➡ **Workbook:** Writing: *A short news article*, page 23

World culture (PAGES 44–45)

Three minutes of exercise

Culture notes

The World Health Organisation (WHO) gives as examples of physical activity things such as walking, dancing, gardening, swimming, cycling, housework, sports and games. For adults aged 18–64, it recommends at least two and a half hours of moderate-intensity aerobic activity per week, or at least 75 minutes of vigorous-intensity exercise, e.g. running. Aerobic activity should be done for at least ten minutes at a time.

Research has clearly indicated that people who follow these recommendations have lower risks of heart disease, high blood pressure, stroke, type 2 diabetes, colon and breast cancer and depression, hip or vertebral fracture. They also have higher levels of fitness and are more likely to be able to maintain a healthy weight.

Find out first (PAGE 44)

1a–b Go through the health benefits with the class, checking understanding where necessary. Students discuss the questions in pairs.

2a If possible, students go online to check their answers using the search terms in the box. Otherwise students check answers with you. Check answers with the class, and feed in information from the Culture notes if necessary.

ANSWERS:

1a All of them are benefits of regular exercise.
 b 150 minutes.

b Students discuss their exercise habits in pairs. If they are comfortable doing so, they can then share their habits with the class.

View (PAGE 44)

See *Teaching tips: Using the video material in the classroom*, page 24.

3a Read the question with the class and elicit students' ideas. Ask if anyone agrees with the statement at this stage and why.

 b ⊙ Go through the summaries with the class, then play the DVD for students to check their answers.

ANSWER:

Summary 2 is correct.

4 Students attempt to answer the questions from memory, then watch the DVD again to check their answers. Check answers with the class.

ANSWERS:

1 F (150 minutes of moderate activity, or 75 minutes of high-intensity activity)
2 F (three minutes a week in total)
3 T
4 F (He says you only need it for traditional exercise.)
5 T
6 T
7 F (He says the last few seconds are really difficult.)

5 Students either discuss this in pairs or as a class.

World view (PAGE 45)

6a ⊙ Go through the things in the box with the class and check students understand them, especially *trans fats* (a type of unsaturated fat in food which can cause heart disease). Play the DVD for students to write who mentions what.

ANSWERS:

Carol: trans fats, fitness areas in parks, pregnant women

George: smoking, saving public spending on health

 b Elicit what students can remember about what they said about each thing, but don't give any answers yet.

7a Students do the exercise from memory in pairs. When they're ready, play the DVD again for them to check answers.

 b Students compare answers in pairs, then check answers with the whole class.

ANSWERS:

1 F (George worries about this, not Carol.)
2 F (He thinks people should have the choice.)
3 F (She asks him to clarify / give an example of what he says.)
4 T
5 T
6 F (She thinks they're a good thing.)
7 T
8 T

8 Put students into groups to discuss the questions. With weaker classes, you could give them a few minutes to first read the questions and make notes of their answers before putting them in groups. When they have finished discussing the questions, nominate a student from each group to share their ideas with the class.

Find out more ⓝ (PAGE 45)

9a Look at the list with the class and elicit what students know, and if anyone has had any experience with any of the regimes or programmes.

 b Students go online alone or in pairs to find out about one of the regimes. Monitor and help with vocabulary where necessary.

Present your research

10 Go through the prompts, eliciting possible endings, and read the Tip with the class. Give students plenty of time to prepare their presentations, and help with vocabulary where necessary. When they are ready, students take turns presenting their findings. Encourage other students to listen and make notes, so that they can ask questions at the end of each presentation.

Students can now do Progress Test 2 on the Teacher's Resource Disc.

Grammar practice (PAGES 126–127)

See *Teaching tips: Using the Grammar and Vocabulary practice sections*, page 25.

Adjectives and adverbs

ANSWERS:

1
1 She has a son from a previous marriage.
2 The cinema was full of frightened people at the premiere of *Night Chills 2*.
3 What seems to be the main reason for his attitude, in your opinion?
4 He tiptoed past the sleeping dog and got himself a biscuit.
5 Do you think that is the only difference between the two tablets?
6 The doctor's waiting room was packed with sick people.

2
1 talented young, spectacular state-of-the-art
2 average monthly, typical American
3 summer outdoor, forthcoming musical
4 charming stone, traditional English

3a
1 an advertisement for accommodation   2 a novel
3 a clothes shop website   4 a TV review   5 a holiday brochure
b
1 This two-bedroom apartment has a good-sized kitchen and a south-facing balcony.
2 Abby smiled as her eight-year-old son tipped out the contents of his schoolbag: a homemade birthday card, a half-eaten apple, a three-day-old sandwich and a pair of mud-covered trainers.
3 Wear this loosely-fitting, long-sleeved shirt with your straight-legged jeans and high-heeled shoes.
4 Don't miss the first episode of the three-part historical drama *Between the Wars*, a thought-provoking story featuring an all-star cast.
5 Discover the delights of Sicily on a five-day tour. Stay in four-star, family-run hotels and sample home-cooked food and local wines. English-speaking representatives are always available to make your stay as easy as possible.

4a
2 un   3 post-   4 dis   5 over   6 mis   7 anti-   8 mal
b
2 maltreated   3 misleading   4 anti-nuclear   5 disconnected
6 post-dated   7 ungrateful   8 overcrowded

5
1 intercontinental   2 dissatisfied   3 pre-owned
4 overrated/underrated   5 overdressed/underdressed
6 antisocial   7 bilingual/multilingual   8 bilingual/monolingual
9 sub-zero   10 multi-purpose

6
(Possible answers)
1 drill, telephone   2 belt   3 tablet computer   4 soft toy, belt
5 tablet computer, telephone
6 everything except a soft toy and a belt
7 drill, tablet computer, washing machine   8 drill

7
1 both options are possible
2 *very stunning*, both options are possible
3 both options are possible, *very delighted*
4 *very unique, absolutely valuable*
5 *the most*

8
Correct: 2, 3, 6, 7
1 I know it's a shabby old jacket, but it's actually pretty/quite comfortable. (*rather comfortable* is also possible, if you want to mean 'more comfortable than I expected')
4 Are you feeling a bit / a little / slightly calmer now?
5 I'm pretty/quite pleased with the amount of work I managed to get done today. (*rather pleased* is possible if you want to mean 'more pleased than I expected')
8 I'm pretty/quite sure that's the turning, coming up on the left.

9
(Possible answers)
1 ingenious   2 little-known   3 lone   4 impressive   5 hugely
6 two-year-old   7 attractive   8 absolutely   9 asleep
10 mind-blowing   11 unique   12 dissatisfied

Vocabulary practice (PAGE 155)

Self-improvement

ANSWERS:

1
1 more *bad* **harm** than good
2 mental *good* **well**-being
3 to *stay* **keep** it up regularly
4 to feel *underwhelmed* **overwhelmed**
5 it really *examines* **tests** your endurance
6 *lengthens* **broadens** your horizons
7 improved your *me* **self**-esteem
8 are purely *psychiatric* **psychological**

Body idioms

ANSWERS:

2
1 stomach   2 eye   3 heart   4 head   5 face   6 nose   7 leg
8 hands

Other words and phrases

ANSWERS:

3
1 metabolic rate   2 lets him down   3 rigorous
4 bored to death   5 manageable targets   6 religiously   7 trim
8 nutritional information

OVERVIEW

PAGES 46–47

Speaking and vocabulary: Polite social behaviour

Common European Framework: Students can express their ideas and opinions with precision; can give a clear, systematically developed presentation, with highlighting of significant points, and relevant supporting detail.

PAGES 48–49

Reading and vocabulary: Image

Grammar review: Modals and related verbs

Common European Framework: Students can obtain information, ideas and opinions from complex texts; can take an active part in informal discussion.

PAGES 50–51

Listening and vocabulary: Communication

Patterns to notice: Patterns with abstract nouns and relative clauses

Common European Framework: Students can understand a wide range of recorded and broadcast audio material and identify finer points of detail; can give clear, detailed descriptions.

PAGES 52–53

Task: Deal with a problem tactfully

Common European Framework: Students can outline an issue or a problem clearly, speculating about causes or consequences, and weighing advantages and disadvantages of different approaches.

PAGES 54–55

Writing: Asking people to do things

Speaking: Getting people to do things

Common European Framework: Students can use language flexibly and effectively for social purposes; can express themselves confidently, clearly and politely in a formal or informal register, appropriate to the situation and person(s) concerned.

Speaking and vocabulary

(PAGES 46–47)

Polite social behaviour

See *Teaching tips: Working with lexis*, page 21.

WARM UP

Before class, prepare to tell the class about a couple of your 'pet peeves', i.e. little things which really annoy you, e.g. people who walk really slowly in front of you, people not saying 'thank you' when you hold the door open for them, etc. Tell the class what they are, why they annoy you and a recent example of when they happened. Give students a few minutes to think of their own 'pet peeves', then put them into groups to tell each other about them. In feedback, ask if anyone had ideas in common.

1 Elicit/Check: *etiquette* (rules about the best way to behave), *private school* versus *state comprehensive school* (private = you pay for it; state comprehensive = the government / taxes pay for it) and *spurred on* (positively encouraged). Students read the text then discuss the questions in pairs. In feedback, elicit students' ideas and have a brief class discussion.

2 This stage can be quite brief, and students should make notes, rather than write complete sentences. Students can compare lists in pairs, small groups, or with the whole class.

3a Go through one or two examples with the class, then put students into pairs or small groups to help each other with the phrases, using a dictionary or their mobile phones if necessary. Check understanding of: *over the top* (informal; meaning so exaggerated as to be stupid or offensive) and *overly familiar* (has a negative meaning in this context; being too friendly when you don't know someone well enough). You may also need to help students with the pronunciation of the following: *awkward* /ˈɔːkwəd/, *familiar* /fəˈmɪliə/, *gentlemanly* /ˈdʒentlmənli/, *unhygienic* /ʌnhaɪˈdʒiːnɪk/ and *misinterpreted* /mɪsɪnˈtɜːprɪtɪd/.

ANSWERS:
It creates a good impression.
It's a way of showing respect to older people.
It's considered gentlemanly.

b Give some examples to show the class how to use the phrases in a sentence, e.g.
It's considered taboo to show anger.
Arriving a few minutes late is the done thing.
Students could work with a different partner to describe some of the ideas from their lists.

4a Give students a few minutes individually to consider how acceptable the situations are. They could make a note of any appropriate vocabulary from exercise 3a, so that they are prepared for the discussion in exercise 4b. Check understanding of *drop in* (visit informally) and *swear* versus *blaspheme* (swear = use offensive language; blaspheme = use language which insults people's religious beliefs).

b Put students into small groups to explain their opinions. Ask a few students to report back on their group's discussion, commenting on the differences between countries, and/or age groups, if appropriate.

5 🎧 5.1 Go over the questions and make sure students know exactly what to listen for. Students listen and make notes, then check in pairs. Play the recording again if necessary, then check answers with the whole class.

ANSWERS:
Speaker 1: When people start talking about the weather.
Speaker 2: When young people use headphones which are too loud.
Speaker 3: When people are late, and text to say 'just running a bit late'.
Speaker 4: When friends spend too much time texting each other on their mobile phones.
Speaker 5: When people snog/kiss in public.

6a Give students time to plan their talks and make a few notes to speak from. Go around and help with ideas and vocabulary, writing any new words/phrases on the board.

b Put students into groups to give their talks. If you have a multilingual class, try to put students from different countries together. While you listen to the talks, make a note of examples of good language use and/or errors for feedback and correction afterwards.

ADDITIONAL PRACTICE

➡ **Resource bank:** Activity 5C *Bad behaviour* (Social behaviour)
Vocabulary practice: Exercise 1
Workbook: Vocabulary: *Polite social behaviour*, pages 24–25

Reading and vocabulary

(PAGES 48–49)

Image

WARM UP

Write the following questions on the board:

How important is your image to you?

What do you do to maintain/improve your image?

For what jobs is image particularly important?

Students discuss the questions in pairs.

1   Students discuss the questions in pairs. In feedback, elicit students' ideas and have a brief class discussion.

> **Reading and vocabulary, exercise 1: Alternative suggestion**
>
> Divide the class into three groups, and assign one of the types of people to each group. Give the groups a few minutes to discuss and write down ideas. When they are ready, rearrange students in groups of three with one student from each of the previous groups. Students share ideas.

2   Students check the meanings of the words in bold in pairs, using dictionaries and/or mobile phones where necessary. Check pronunciation of: *Botox* /ˈbəʊtɒks/, *posture* /ˈpɒstʃə/ and *charisma* /kəˈrɪzmə/.

3   Elicit/Check: *hip* (trendy), *love handles* (fat on a person's hips/ waist) and *an entourage* (a group of personal assistants who follow a celebrity around, looking after him/her). Encourage the students to read the text quickly, and explain that they'll have a chance to read it again more carefully afterwards. Give students three minutes to match the headings and paragraphs, then check answers with the class.

> **ANSWERS:**
>
> **1** b   **2** c   **3** f   **4** a   **5** e

4   Students answer the questions alone then check in pairs, before checking answers with the whole class.

> **ANSWERS:**
>
> **Paragraph 1: a** true, **b** true
>
> **Paragraph 2: a** true, **b** true
>
> **Paragraph 3: b** true
>
> **Paragraph 4: b** true, **c** true
>
> **Paragraph 5: a** true, **b** true, **c** true

5   Put students into groups to discuss the questions. When they have finished, choose a student from each group to summarise their ideas for the class.

ADDITIONAL PRACTICE

➡ **Workbook:** Vocabulary: *Image*, page 25

Grammar review (PAGE 49)

Modals and related verbs

See *Teaching tips: Using a discovery approach to grammar*, page 20.

1   Elicit which modals students know and write them on the board, e.g. *can/could, may/might, will/would, shall/should, must*. Do the first one together as an example, then students do the rest alone before checking in pairs. Encourage them to look back at how the sentences are used in the text. Check answers with the class.

> **ANSWERS:**
>
> **1** can (h)   **2** mustn't (b)   **3** had to (c), could (e)   **4** can (i)
> **5** might (d)   **6** won't (g)   **7** needn't (j)   **8** should (a)
> **9** must (f)

2   Discuss the rules as a class.

> **ANSWERS:**
>
> **1** a speaker's opinion   **2** regular   **3** irregular

3   Go through the first one as an example. Students work in pairs to discuss the differences between the rest. Check answers with the class.

> **ANSWERS:**
>
> **2** Both talk about logical necessity. In both cases, the speaker is making a deduction based on some kind of evidence; *must* means 'I believe it's true' and *can't* means 'I believe it's impossible'.
> **3** Both talk about ability. *Could* refers to general ability in the past, whereas *managed to* refers to one specific occasion.
> **4** Both talk about necessity. *Didn't need to* means that there was no need, and the speaker didn't do this. *Needn't have* means that the speaker did do this, even though there was no need.
> **5** Both talk about advice. There is little difference in meaning, although we are much more likely to say *shouldn't* than *oughtn't to*.
> **6** Both talk about unwillingness. However, *won't* talks generally about what people don't do, wheras *wouldn't* talks about a specific refusal in the past.

You may want to ask students to read Language summary 5 on pages 128–129 for a more detailed explanation of modals and related verbs.

ADDITIONAL PRACTICE

➡ **Resource bank:** Activity 5A *Guess the sentence* (Modals and related verbs)

Grammar practice: Exercises 1–9

Workbook: Grammar: *Modals and related verbs*, page 27

Listening and vocabulary

(PAGES 50–51)

Communication

1 Focus students on the statistics and discuss briefly their ideas about why people are shy and why it can be a problem (note that *chronically* is used for a problem you have had for a long time and cannot stop). Ask them why they think people want to improve their communication skills.

2 Students choose their situations individually then compare answers in pairs. Check understanding of: *fancy someone* (feel sexually attracted to someone) and *light-hearted* (not serious)

> **Listening and vocabulary, exercise 2: Alternative suggestions**
>
> a You could deal with the vocabulary in exercise 3a before starting the pairwork in exercise 2, so that students can talk about how they would feel and what they would do at the same time.
>
> b You could write out the situations on separate slips of paper, and give a set to each group: students then try to agree on an order from the most to least nerve-wracking and arrange the slips accordingly.

3a To check the meaning of the activities, you could ask students which are to do with speaking, and which are to do with the way you hold or move your body. While students are working, go around and help with any vocabulary questions they have.

b Students compare answers in pairs and discuss the statements.

> **POSSIBLE ANSWERS:**
>
> **Good:** circulate and make small talk; ask questions and make the other people feel at ease; make eye contact; pause from time to time; listen carefully
>
> **Not good:** gabble nervously about whatever comes into your head; dry up because you can't think of anything to say; talk over other people and dominate the conversation; become over-apologetic; giggle nervously; stumble over your words; get emotional; look stiff and uncomfortable; blush, shake or sweat
>
> **Depends:** crack lots of jokes; act cool and nonchalant

4 🎧 **5.2** Introduce the idea of a communication skills expert and go through questions 1 and 2 before playing the recording.

> **ANSWERS:**
>
> Rosemary refers to: socialising at a party where you only know one or two people; talking about a subject you don't know much about; socialising for the evening with a group of people you feel are senior to you; making a complaint.

5 Give students time to remember what they can, then ask them to make notes as they listen again.

> **ANSWERS:**
>
> 1 This is true, because they feel that the other person won't be interested in them.
> 2 Rosemary said you should ask some, but not too many or it will sound like an interrogation.
> 3 She said you should pause to allow the other person to reflect upon what you have said and to give you time to think about what you will say next.
> 4 You may give the message that you like them too much, or come across as aggressive.
> 5 You should listen actively to the other person.
> 6 It helps to summarise or test your understanding of what they have said.
> 7 Many people need to work on communication skills.

PATTERNS TO NOTICE

Patterns with abstract nouns and relative clauses

1 & 2 Put the first two example sentences on the board and point out the abstract nouns (*situations* and *the way*) and the relative pronouns (*where* and *which/that*). Then students can look at the list of examples and pick out the abstract nouns and relative pronouns.

Students complete the sentences alone then check in pairs, before checking answers with the whole class.

> **ANSWERS:**
>
> 1 why   2 where   3 where   4 why   5 which   6 which
> 7 where

> **Patterns to notice: Alternative suggestions**
>
> To help students to notice the noun / relative pronoun collocations:
>
> a Students can 'test' each other in pairs. Student A reads out the first half of a sentence up to the abstract noun, and student B has to give the correct relative pronoun without looking at the book, e.g. Student A '*There are many reasons …*' Student B '*why*'.
>
> b Write out the sentences on slips of paper and cut them in half after the abstract noun. In pairs, students have to match the sentence halves, e.g. *We have seen several cases / where people have started arguing.*

6 Students work individually then compare answers in pairs and/or with the whole class.

> **ANSWERS:**
>
> 2 There are various reasons why nervous people forget to smile.
> 3 I have seen many situations where people talk too much because they are nervous.
> 4 It is quite common to come across cases where two people remember different things from the same conversation.
> 5 There are a large number of reasons (for) why people dread long conversations with senior colleagues at parties.
> 6 It is essential to have a time where everyone can calm down after an argument.
> 7 People often judge you unconsciously on the way you stand or sit while you are talking.
> 8 Many people respond negatively to the way in which / that people complain.

7a Give one or two examples from your own life in order to demonstrate the activity. While students are writing their sentences, go around and help with vocabulary where necessary, writing any new words/phrases on the board.

b Go through the example with the class. Students read out their sentences in pairs for their partner to guess. In feedback, nominate students to tell you something interesting they found out about their partner.

ADDITIONAL PRACTICE

➡ **Resource bank:** Activity 5B *Abstract descriptions* (Patterns with abstract nouns and relative clauses); Activity 5D *It's how I tell them* (Communication)

Vocabulary practice: Exercises 2a–b

Workbook: Listen and read: *Nosey questions*, page 26; Vocabulary: *Communication*, page 27; Grammar: *Patterns with abstract nouns and relative clauses*, page 27

Task (PAGES 52–53)

Deal with a problem tactfully

See *Teaching tips: Making tasks work*, page 23.

WARM UP

Write the following on the board:
Your colleague at work is taking the credit for work you've done.
You suspect your partner is cheating on you.
You aren't happy in your job, but can't afford to leave right now.
Your best friend has a hygiene problem.

Put students into pairs to put the problems in order from the easiest to the worst to deal with, and discuss how they would handle each one. In feedback, nominate students to share their ideas with the class.

Preparation (PAGES 52–53)

Reading and vocabulary

1   You could lead into this by asking students what kinds of topics personal problems are usually related to, e.g. family, romantic relationships, work, studies, health, money. Students can discuss the responses in pairs or small groups.

2   Elicit/Check: *fly off the handle* (informal; get angry suddenly about something that doesn't seem very important), *be at your wits' end* (be very worried), *land a job* (informal; succeed in getting a job that was difficult to get), *be besotted with someone* (be completely in love with someone) and *washed-out* (looking unhealthy). Focus students on the titles and accompanying photos for the three situations and encourage them to try to predict what the problem is in each case. Give them time to read through the situations to see if their predictions were correct and find out new information about each problem.

> **Preparation: Alternative suggestions**
>
> a   If you have short lessons, choose just one of the situations for students to read and discuss, i.e. whichever you feel they will identify with best.
>
> b   If your students enjoy being creative, put them into groups to invent and write about a problem situation themselves, then each group passes the situation to another group for discussion at the Task stage. They could use one of the situations given as a model, so that they make the problem complex enough to generate plenty of discussion.
>
> c   If you want to make this a listening activity and have access to video, use an episode from an English-speaking TV soap opera where one of the characters has a difficult problem.

Task (PAGES 52–53)

Speaking

1a   You could start by finding out which situations your students identify with, e.g. because they know someone who this has happened to / could happen to, or because they could imagine being in that situation themselves. Divide students into groups according to the situation they choose (the groups do not all need to be of the same size).

b   While students are considering the options individually, circulate and help with vocabulary as necessary, writing any new words/phrases on the board.

2   Focus students on the Useful language box, sections a and b before they start the discussion. You may want to go through some examples of how to complete the phrases, e.g.
The main thing to get across is that it's her decision.
One way to tackle it might be to get him away from the family for a while.
Speaking to his father wouldn't go down too well.

Encourage students to make notes during the discussion about which options they decided against / in favour of, and why. While you monitor this discussion, you could make notes of good language use and/or errors for feedback and correction later.

3   You could either ask two students from each group to present their conclusions to the class (e.g. one student presents the options they decided against, the other presents the options they decided would be best) or regroup students so that each group contains people who have discussed different problems, and students present their conclusions to the group.

> **Task: Additional activity**
>
> Once students have finished discussing the best and worst options, they role-play two scenarios – one where the problem is tackled badly, the other where it is tackled well – then present these to the rest of the class. Note that students can then choose to write up one of the scenarios for the Follow up, Writing stage.

Follow up (PAGE 53)

Writing

1   Refer students to the Useful language box, section c.

For option a, when students have finished, ask them to swap and read other students' responses and choose the best one.

For option b, you could start by writing one or two example lines for a script on the board, showing students how stage directions can be put in brackets, e.g. *(Anna bursts into tears and runs out of the room)*. Students can work in pairs on their script (you may want to give them a number of lines to aim for, so that it is not too long) and practise reading it aloud. As they watch each other's scenes, students could give 'awards', e.g. for 'best script', 'best acting', 'best English pronunciation', etc.

> **Task: Additional suggestion**
>
> Students write a final draft of the posting or play script they wrote in Follow up, Writing, exercise 1, if they haven't done so in class.

> **Share your task**
>
> Some additional ideas could include:
>
> - Students prepare their scene in the style of a daytime television talk show where people confront other people with problems.
> - Students think of another personal problem, not covered on pages 52–53, then film/record themselves as the person with the problem. Other students then watch/listen to the recording and give advice.
> - Students film/record themselves giving advice for one of the situations on pages 52–53. Other students then listen to or watch the recording and guess which problem they're giving advice for.

Language live (PAGES 54–55)

Writing (PAGES 54–55)
Asking people to do things

1a Students read the three emails then check answers in pairs. In feedback, check answers and answer any questions students have about new vocabulary in the emails.

POSSIBLE ANSWERS:
A They are friends.
B They are colleagues, working in the same place.
C A student is writing to a PR expert she has never met.

b Students choose the phrases to complete the emails in pairs. Check answers with the class.

ANSWERS:
1 a & c (b is too formal)
2 b & c (a is too formal)
3 a & b (c is too formal)
4 a & b (c is too formal)
5 b & c (a is too direct)
6 a & b (c is inappropriate, as there is nothing to 'see')
7 a & c (b could sound rude, as it is too direct)
8 b & c (a is too informal)
9 b & c (a is too informal and direct)
10 b & c (a is too informal)

Notes on email

People are often unsure how to sign off an email, especially if they want to be semi-formal or neutral. What makes it more difficult is that this seems to change quite often, even for native speakers. It could be useful here to look back over your own email inbox and collect a variety of ways people have signed off when writing to you, then share them with the class. The students are likely to appreciate the fact that these have been taken from real emails.

2 Do this as a class. As you go through each strategy, ask students if the same applies in their language(s).

3 Students discuss this in pairs. When they are ready, check answers with the class and write any other useful phrases students identify on the board.

ANSWERS:
A 2, 5   B 1, 5   C 2, 3, 4, 5, 6

4 Put students into groups of three, but explain that they'll work alone to write their replies. Give students five minutes to write brief replies. When they are ready, students compare replies within their group. In feedback, ask students to share their best examples with the class.

5 If you feel they would benefit from more practice, students can write all three emails.

6a Refer students back to the phrases/strategies from exercises 1 and 2 and encourage them to use these when checking their partner's work.

b Students write their second drafts, either in class or for homework. You could ask them to email the finished versions to you.

Speaking (PAGE 55)
Getting people to do things

1 🎧 **5.3** Focus students on the pictures and give them a few minutes to discuss the situations. They could also predict what the people will actually say, then listen and see how close their versions were.

ANSWERS:
Picture A: She wants him to move to another seat so a family can sit together.
Picture B: She wants him to pick up her dry cleaning.
Picture C: She wants her colleague to help her print something.
Picture D: He wants the customer not to use his mobile phone in the restaurant.

2a You could do an example with the class: ask students to identify the person speaking from the pictures in exercise 1, and to decide why the phrase is being used.

ANSWERS:
1 Are you in the middle of … ? ; Shall I come back later?; Sorry to disturb you.
2 Can I ask a really, really big favour?; I wonder if you might be able to help.; I'd be really grateful.; We would very much appreciate it.; I must ask you not to …
3 I don't see why I should.
4 I'll be right with you.; If you'll just bear with me for a minute.
5 Oh, all right then.; Oh, go on.

b 🎧 **5.4** Either play the recording or say the phrases naturally yourself, for students to practise the intonation. Point out that intonation often conveys the speaker's attitude more clearly than the actual words they use.

3a You may want to play the conversations again, stopping after each one for students to describe the speakers' attitudes.

ANSWERS:
Picture A: annoyed, uncooperative
Picture B: reluctant, casual
Picture C: cooperative, polite
Picture D: extremely polite, cooperative

b Students can discuss the language in the audio script in pairs.

ANSWERS:
Conversation A: Are you in the middle of something?; Well, shall I come back later?; Sorry to disturb you.; Thanks … sorry to be a nuisance.
Conversation B: Can I ask a really, really big favour?; Oh, go on.
Conversation C: May I disturb you for one moment?; Would that be at all possible?; We would very much appreciate it if you could help us here.
Conversation D: I must ask you not to use your mobile phone … ; Thank you, sir.

4 Put students into pairs to prepare a similar conversation to the ones in exercise 1. Encourage them to use phrases from exercise 2 where appropriate, and to discuss the questions to help them prepare. When students have prepared their conversations, they take turns acting them out for the class.

Speaking, exercise 4: Alternative suggestion

If you are short of time, students choose one of the four situations on the recording to rewrite, changing the attitude of one of the speakers, and/or the outcome of the conversation.

Students can now do the Mid-course test on the Teacher's Resource Disc.

ADDITIONAL PRACTICE

→ **Workbook:** Writing: *Asking people to do things*, page 28; Language live: *Getting people to do things*, page 28

Grammar practice (PAGES 130–131)

See *Teaching tips: Using the Grammar and Vocabulary practice sections*, page 25.

Modals

ANSWERS:

1
1 There is no difference in meaning.
2 Both sentences can mean 'it's possible that he went home early', but *could have* can also mean 'it was possible for him to go home early, but he didn't'.
3 There is a difference in meaning: *can take* means it's generally possible, whereas *could take* refers to a specific possibility, either in the past, present or future.
4 There is a difference in meaning: *should win* means probably, whereas *could win* means it is possible.
5 Both sentences can mean 'it's possible that they got stuck in traffic', but *could have* can also mean 'it was possible for them to get stuck in traffic, but they didn't'.

2
1 wouldn't eat   2 couldn't even get up   3 could see
4 was able to remove   5 Benji could have died   6 Benji should be

4
1 ~~would~~   2 ~~would~~   3 all three are possible   4 ~~Will~~   5 ~~May~~
6 all three are possible   7 ~~Will~~   8 ~~may~~

5
(Possible answers)
1 Can I pay by credit card?
2 Can/May I go out now?
3 Can/Could/Will/Would you do the washing-up?
4 Can/Could I borrow your car?
5 Could/May I see Mr Davidson?
6 Can/Could/Will/Would you look after my dog for me?

6
1 must be presented (written)
2 can't have seen (spoken)
3 must not leave (written)
4 will/must be waiting (spoken); *will be waiting* implies certainty, whereas *must be waiting* implies a logical deduction
5 mustn't/shouldn't eat (spoken); *mustn't* is stronger than *shouldn't*, which means 'it's not a good idea'
6 must have gone (spoken)
7 will / should / have got to pay (spoken); *will pay* describes an intention made at the time of speaking, *should pay* means 'it's a good idea', and *have got to pay* describes an obligation
8 must/should be switched off (written); *must be switched off* describes an obligation, *should be switched off* describes a suggestion

7
1 You mustn't miss the United game on Saturday.
2 The management must act quickly to prevent bullying in the workplace.
3 How long did you have to wait for your new passport?
4 Do you have to carry an ID card in your country?
5 Ring Alvaro later – he won't have had time to unpack yet.
6 You shouldn't have invited Ali without asking me.
7 That must be Zoe's book – she's just phoned up about it.
8 You must have driven like a maniac to get here so quickly!

8
1 has to
2 needs
3 dare
4 ought to have
5 needn't / don't have to
6 don't have to
7 having to
8 didn't dare (to) / had to; *didn't dare to* means he didn't have the courage to admit it, *had to* means he had no choice
9 needn't have
10 dared

9
1 d   2 g   3 a   4 b   5 f   6 h   7 c   8 i   9 e

Vocabulary practice (PAGE 156)

Polite social behaviour

ANSWERS:

1
1 pushy   2 coughing, sneezing   3 gentlemanly   4 impression
5 yawning   6 familiar   7 drop in   8 over the top   9 awkward
10 rowing

Communication

ANSWERS:

2
1 f +   2 d −   3 j −   4 a +   5 h −   6 e +   7 l −   8 b −   9 g −
10 k +   11 i +   12 c +

Other words and phrases

ANSWERS:

3
1 get defensive   2 face facts   3 Pull yourself together
4 supportive   5 patronising   6 close up

OVERVIEW

PAGES 56–57

Vocabulary and speaking: Education

Common European Framework: Students can understand enough to follow extended speech on abstract topics; can easily follow and contribute to group discussion.

PAGES 58–59

Reading and vocabulary: Learning

Grammar review: Use and non-use of the passive

Common European Framework: Students can understand in detail a wide range of complex texts; can summarise and give their opinion about an article.

PAGES 60–61

Listening and speaking: Experiences of education

Patterns to notice: Particles which modify the meaning of verbs

Pronunciation: Stress patterns with verbs and particles

Common European Framework: Students can follow extended speech even when it is not clearly structured; can place stress correctly.

PAGES 62–63

Task: Teach a practical skill

Common European Framework: Students can give a clear, detailed description of how to carry out a procedure.

PAGES 64–65

World culture: Teaching happiness

Common European Framework: Students can understand a wide range of recorded and broadcast audio material; can give a clear, well-structured presentation of a complex subject.

Vocabulary and speaking

(PAGES 56–57)

Education

See *Teaching tips: Working with lexis*, page 21.

WARM UP

Draw a word web on the board with *school subjects* in the middle. Elicit as many school subjects as you can from the class. Students discuss which are/were their (least) favourite subjects and why.

1   Students should close their books or cover page 57. Demonstrate writing one or two words next to the letter 'a' on the board, e.g. *arithmetic, art, algebra*. Put students into small groups and set the two-minute time limit.

> **Vocabulary and speaking, exercise 1: Alternative suggestion**
>
> To add an element of competition, as you go through the answers, give one point for every relevant word and two bonus points for a relevant word that nobody else thought of.

2a–b   Students can work in pairs or small groups to help each other complete the quiz, then check their answers on page 107. Be prepared to give further explanations/examples where necessary.

> **Notes on vocabulary**
>
> In British English, both *public* and *private schools* are schools which you pay to go to. *State schools* are free and paid for by the government / taxes.
>
> In US English, *private schools* are privately funded while *public schools* are funded by the government / taxes.

3   Students work individually to mark the statements as true or false for their country/ies.

> **Vocabulary and speaking, exercise 3: Alternative suggestion**
>
> If your students are all from the same country and are likely to have very similar answers, ask them to think about whether or not the statements are true of other countries. They can then go online to check answers.

4   When they have finished, students work in pairs to compare answers. Encourage students to ask follow-up questions, e.g. *'In my country, classes in schools are quite small.' 'Really? How many pupils are there in a typical class?'*

5   🎧 **6.1** Play the recording for students to identify the statements and note the opinions given. Students check in pairs before checking answers with the whole class.

> **ANSWERS:**
>
> **Speaker 1:** University fees are very high; putting a limit on people for education because of money is completely unfair.
>
> **Speaker 2:** Students do a huge number of exams, retakes, etc.; children need time to experiment, play and enjoy life.
>
> **Speaker 3:** Children start school too early; they need to be at home to develop their own sense of identity for as long as possible.
>
> **Speaker 4:** Class sizes in schools and universities are very large; if you had smaller class sizes, the children would learn a lot more.

6   Students discuss some of the statements in pairs. In feedback, nominate students to share their ideas with the class and have a brief class discussion.

> **Vocabulary and speaking, exercise 6: Additional activity**
>
> Students discuss which new subjects they'd like to introduce at school, e.g. driving lessons, shopping tips, etc.

ADDITIONAL PRACTICE

➡ **Resource bank:** Activity 6C *Education crossword* (Education)
   Vocabulary practice: Exercise 1
   Workbook: Vocabulary: *Education*, page 30

Reading and vocabulary

(PAGES 58–59)

Learning

See *Teaching tips: Working with lexis*, page 21.

1   Focus attention on the statements and check understanding. Students discuss in groups. When they are ready, have a class vote via show of hands and write students' predictions on the board.

2 Elicit/Check: *shrink* (get smaller), *cork* (what we use to close a wine bottle) and *be hampered by something* (face a difficulty). Encourage students to read quickly, explaining that they'll have a chance to read the articles more carefully afterwards. Students check answers in pairs before checking with the whole class.

> **ANSWERS:**
> **A** 3 The more you praise a child, the better. (The article says the opposite may be true.)
> **B** 2 Stress is bad for the brain.
> **C** 4 Humans are always more intelligent than animals. (The article summarises research which suggests that some animals are as intelligent as children up to the age of eight.)

3 Students read again and check the statements alone, then check in pairs. In feedback, ask students to tell you which part of the text proves/disproves each statement.

> **ANSWERS:**
> **Article A: a** false, **b** true, **c** true
> **Article B: a** false, **b** false, **c** true
> **Article C: a** false, **b** true, **c** true

4 Direct students to the appropriate pages and encourage them to take notes on a separate piece of paper when answering the questions.

> **ANSWERS:**
> **Student A**
> **1** We can all have extraordinary mental abilities if we switch off a part of our brain.
> **2** It switches off the conscious part of the brain.
> **3** That some people seem to perform better in calculation or drawing tasks.
> **4** Some people may experience future side-effects which actually make their mental abilities worse.
> **Student B**
> **1** The subject was primary school children in the Netherlands.
> **2** That many children have serious worries.
> **3** Being away from their parents for a long time, or being stressed at school.
> **4** Spending more time with their parents.

5a–b Ask students to close their books, but allow them to look at the notes they made when summarising their articles. When they have finished, ask students to look at their partner's text and see if they summarised it accurately. In feedback, elicit what students found interesting about what they read.

> **Reading and vocabulary, exercises 4 & 5: Alternative suggestion**
> When students are summarising what they have read, ask them to include one small piece of false information. When they read the other texts in exercise 5b, students try and work out what the false piece of information was.

6 Students discuss the questions in groups. When they have finished, nominate a student from each group to share their ideas with the class.

ADDITIONAL PRACTICE

Resource bank: Activity 6D *What is it?* (Learning)
Vocabulary practice: Exercise 2
Workbook: Listen and read: *Distance learning*, page 29; Vocabulary: *Learning*, page 30

Grammar review (PAGE 59)

Use and non-use of the passive

See *Teaching tips: Using a discovery approach to grammar*, page 20.

1a Students choose the correct answers alone then check in pairs.

b Make sure students understand that they should also look at the article on page 108. In feedback, elicit answers and ask why each one is correct. This should give you an idea of how much the students already know about forming the passive.

> **ANSWERS:**
> **1** It is generally believed   **2** were, allowed   **3** being   **4** gone
> **5** conducted   **6** was dropped   **7** by   **8** to be   **9** be, being
> **10** getting
> Sentences 4 (*having gone*) and 9 (*being stressed*) contain non-passive forms.

2a Students work in pairs before checking answers with the class.

> **ANSWERS:**
> **a past:** *were praised, were allowed, conducted, was dropped*
> **present:** *it is generally believed, being tested, are hampered, are known, could be caused, getting assessed*
> **b** *being tested, getting assessed*
> **c** *could be caused*
> **d** *to be caused*
> **e** *conducted* (the full form is *which was conducted*)
> **f** *getting assessed*

b Students work in pairs. In feedback, elicit answers and be prepared to give further explanations where necessary.

> **ANSWERS:**
> **a** 1, 3, 4, 8, 9   **b** 2, 5, 6, 7   **c** 1, 3, 4, 8   **d** 1

> **Potential problem with the passive**
> Students may want to use *by* to introduce the subject where it isn't necessary, especially if they have learnt the passive in a more traditional, mechanical way by focusing more on the form than the use. This might lead to some strange examples, such as *The camera was stolen by a thief*. Make sure that students understand we only use *by* if the information is important, and we need to keep the focus on the object, e.g. *My favourite book is 'Bleak House' which was written by Dickens*. (because the focus is on the book).

You may want to ask students to read Language summary 6 on pages 132–133 for a more detailed explanation of use and non-use of the passive.

3a Elicit an example or two from the class if necessary. Give students plenty of time to complete the sentences, and go around checking they're forming them correctly.

b Students compare sentences in pairs. Encourage them to ask/answer follow-up questions to find out more information.

ADDITIONAL PRACTICE

Resource bank: Activity 6A *Which is the best way?* (Use and non-use of the passive)
Grammar practice: Exercises 1–8
Workbook: Grammar: *Use and non-use of the passive*, pages 30–32

Listening and speaking (PAGES 60–61)

Experiences of education

WARM UP

Write on the board: *My education was ...* and ask students to write one sentence to sum up how they feel about their education. Monitor and help with vocabulary where needed. When they are ready, put students into groups to compare ideas.

1a Give students a minute or two to read the comments, and help with any vocabulary where necessary.

b Students discuss the questions in pairs. In feedback, elicit students' ideas and have a brief class discussion.

> **ANSWERS:**
> **Positive:** My education was very well rounded and gave me a broad outlook on life. / It was really fun, creative and motivating. / I think my education really helped to make me focused and hard-working.
> **Negative:** The approach was very traditional; lots of rote learning and tests. / Bullying was a real problem at my school. / We didn't learn much that was useful in real life.
> **Either:** Discipline was strict - there were loads of rules. / My education helped to make me self-motivated and able to learn things for myself. The whole experience made me and a lot of other people feel rather aimless. / It made you very mature and adult.

2 Discuss the questions as a class, and write students' guesses on the board.

3a 🎧 **6.2** Students listen and take notes. Don't go through any answers yet.

b 🎧 **6.3** Play the recording for students to make notes about Eva and Lester.

c Students compare answers in pairs. If necessary, play the recordings again before checking answers with the whole class.

> **ANSWERS:**
> **Gina:** learnt normal subjects like English and maths alongside vocational classes like singing or ballet. She had an amazing time and there was little bullying. She thinks she became mature very quickly, because she started earning money at a young age. However, she thinks that some pupils lost a bit of their childhood because they were already worrying about work, and perhaps their education suffered a bit.
> **Steve:** went to a boarding school at a young age. There were lots of rules and traditions, as well as an old-fashioned uniform. There was little free time, even at the weekend. However, this did help Steve to focus on goals, and learn how to deal with busy schedules.
> **Eva:** became fluent in English and French at a young age. She had lots of friends from different countries. However, she felt a little bit separated, because she was the only Polish person there.
> **Lester:** studied at home. He liked being able to direct his own studies, and being able to focus in depth on what he wanted. He taught himself how to learn at a young age. However, when he went to university, he found the complex social life difficult at first.

4 Students discuss the questions in groups. Check answers to the first question with the class.

> **ANSWERS:**
> **Gina:** It made you very mature and adult.
> **Steve:** Discipline was strict – there were loads of rules. / The approach was very traditional; lots of rote learning and tests.
> **Eva:** My education was very well rounded and gave me a broad outlook on life.
> **Lester:** My education helped to make me self-motivated and able to learn things for myself. The whole experience made me and a lot of other people feel rather aimless.

PATTERNS TO NOTICE

Particles which modify the meaning of verbs
With weaker classes, you may want to get students to do exercise 5 before looking at the information in the box, so that they have already seen some examples of the effect that particles have on the meaning of verbs. With stronger classes, you could write up the particles on the board first and elicit some examples, before they look at the chart.

1a–b Write the examples on the board, and elicit students' ideas as to what meaning the particles add.

2a–b Students read and check their answers to section 1. Go through the examples in the tables, and check understanding by eliciting a further example for each one.

5 Discuss the first one with the class as an example. Students discuss the others in pairs, before checking answers with the whole class.

> **ANSWERS:**
> **1** *around* = pointless activity / in the vicinity (of home)
> **2** *down* = onto paper
> **3** *off* = to another place
> **4** *on* = continue
> **5** *out* = loudly/publicly
> **6** *out* = to different people
> **7** *up* = complete/finish
> **8** *off* = to another place

6 Students work alone then check in pairs, before checking answers with the whole class.

> **ANSWERS:**
> **1** took down **2** went off
> **3** given me my book back / given me back my book
> **4** spoke out **5** eat up

7a Elicit the first answer as an example. Students complete the questions alone then check in pairs. Check answers with the class.

> **ANSWERS:**
> **1** write down / note down **2** rush off / run away **3** tidy up
> **4** hung around **5** send your CV out **6** speak out **7** calm down
> **8** move away

b Students ask and answer the questions in pairs. In feedback, ask questions to share any interesting information with the class.

8a 🎧 **6.4** Play the recording, pausing after each sentence for students to write it down. Give students a chance to check answers in pairs then play the recording again if necessary. Check answers with the class.

> **ANSWERS:**
> **1** I need to talk to you. Don't rush off!
> **2** You're walking far too fast for me. Can't you slow down?
> **3** I'm not waiting any longer. I'm sick of hanging around!
> **4** Can you put your hands up, please? Don't shout out!
> **5** We need to get moving, guys. Eat up!
> **6** Those two seem to be getting on well. Look, they're chatting away!
> **7** Have you finished with that? Can you put it back?
> **8** OK everyone, get out your pens. Write this down.

b Students listen again, paying attention to the stressed particles. Pause after each sentence for students to repeat.

ADDITIONAL PRACTICE

➡ **Resource bank:** Activity 6B *Particle dominoes* (Particles which modify the meaning of verbs)

Workbook: Grammar: *Particles which modify meaning*, page 32

Task (PAGES 62–63)

Teach a practical skill

See *Teaching tips: Making tasks work*, page 23.

If possible, spread the *Preparation* and *Task* over two lessons, so students have time to prepare and find the necessary props and/or diagrams for Task, exercise 1b.

WARM UP

Write the following on the board: *back, up, down, out, around, away, on*. Read out the following for students to guess the verb + particle:
'Blank' 'blank' to when you were a child. Did you enjoy school? ('*Think back*')
Where's your favourite place to 'blank' 'blank' with friends? ('*hang around*')
Would you consider 'blanking' 'blank' to a new area for a job? ('*moving away*')
Students then think of and write a question using one of the particles on the board. Go around and help where necessary. When they are ready, students walk around asking and answering their questions.

Preparation (PAGE 62)

Vocabulary and listening

1a Students could compare their answers in small groups, or walk around the class and talk to others. Then students can report back on how many people in the group/class can do each skill.

b Students match the words/phrases to the skills in groups. Encourage them to use dictionaries and/or mobile phones to look up unfamiliar words. In feedback, check answers and give further explanations where necessary.

ANSWERS:
spare tyre 7, 9; focal point 1, 2; clutch 3; jack 9; press down 1, 8;
turn something upside down 2, 4, 7; special lens 1; crease 4;
ignition 3; collar and cuffs 4; support the head 6, 8;
pump (something) up 7; bubbles 6; cuticles 10; patch 7;
inner tube 7; crop 2; toss 5

2a Give students time to put the pictures in order. Don't give any answers at this stage.

b 🎧 **6.5** Play the recording for students to check their answers to exercise 2a. Use the words in the box to elicit what else students can remember.

ANSWERS:
centre right, centre left, bottom left, top left, top right, bottom right

3a–b Explain that students are going to explain how to give CPR. Ask if they want to listen again before doing so, and if so, play the recording once more. Students practise explaining how to give CPR in pairs.

Preparation, exercise 3: Alternative suggestions

Instead of using the recording:

a Provide the model yourself. To keep this as natural as possible, prepare some notes to refer to, but do not script the explanation. Try to incorporate some of the Useful language at relevant points, so that students can tick off the phrases they hear you use. It would also be a good idea to bring in some props and diagrams to illustrate your skill. You could show these to students before you start, and see if they can predict which skill you are going to talk about.

b If you know someone (e.g. another teacher in the school), who is an expert in one of the skills, ask them to come in and talk to the students. As above, ask them to speak fairly spontaneously from notes rather than a script, and to bring in props and/or diagrams. If it is not possible for the person to visit the class, you could film/record them and show this to the students.

Task (PAGE 63)

Speaking

1a Emphasise that students should choose a skill that they know well, otherwise their talk will be too short. Circulate and advise students on their choices.

b Go through the phrases in the Useful language box, sections a and b. Circulate while students prepare their talks, helping with vocabulary and encouraging them to practise their talks with you. Note that if you are spreading the task over two lessons, students can do this preparation for homework, and prepare props and/or diagrams as necessary. In the next lesson they can practise with a partner, as a 'dry run', before the next stage.

2 To help students decide which talks and skills they want to listen to, put a list of all the students' names and skills on the board. Then ask students to choose two skills, and check that everybody will have an 'audience' (you may have to persuade some students to change their minds). Refer students to the Useful language box, section c for phrases to check understanding. Encourage students to write questions while they are listening to each skill, so they can ask the speaker afterwards. While you are listening to the explanations, you could note down examples of good language use and/or errors for feedback and correction later.

Task, exercise 2: Alternative suggestions

a If your class is too big to have students moving around as suggested, put students into groups of four or five to give their explanations, ensuring that there is a variety of different skills in each group.

b If you have a small class, students can take turns to give their explanation to the whole class. Afterwards, each student can report back on the explanation they found most useful or interesting.

Follow up (PAGE 63)

Writing

1 This could be done in class or for homework. Students could use this as an opportunity to find out more about a skill they know less about, by first researching it online.

Share your task

Some additional ideas could include:

- Students prepare a worksheet and/or some comprehension questions to accompany their talk. Other students watch/listen and complete the worksheet.

- Students film/record themselves as part of a 'How to ...' radio or TV programme.

- Students record themselves, but don't say what it is they're explaining. Other students listen and guess what it is.

- Students film/record themselves, and include one false instruction. Other students watch/listen and guess what it is.

ADDITIONAL PRACTICE

➡ **Workbook:** Writing: *Teaching a practical skill*, page 33

World culture (PAGES 64–65)

Teaching happiness

Culture notes

Subjective Well-Being (SWB) is a measurement of how satisfied people are with specific areas of their lives and how they feel emotionally. It is measured by self-questionnaires and other methods. There are two main theories about what affects SWB: a *top-down* perspective, which says people's happiness is affected by their genetic make-up, and a *bottom-up* perspective, which states that happiness is affected by the experiences a person has. There are also a number of other factors taken into account which can affect SWB, including social influences, wealth, health (mental and physical) and culture. As of 2013, the five countries with the highest levels of happiness (in order) are: 1 Denmark, 2 Norway, 3 Switzerland, 4 the Netherlands and 5 Sweden.

Find out first (PAGE 64)

1   Go through the questions with the class, then ask them to go online and check answers, using the search terms given. When they have found the information, students check in pairs before checking with the whole class. As you elicit what they've found out, feed in information from the Culture notes.

ANSWERS:
1 SWB is a measure of how people experience their lives.
2 Denmark, Norway, Switzerland, the Netherlands and Sweden
3 **a** 40%, 15%; **b** doubled; **c** decreases; **d** 11%

2   Students discuss the questions in groups. When they are ready, elicit ideas and have a brief class discussion.

View (PAGE 64)

See *Teaching tips: Using the video material in the classroom*, page 24.

3   ⏵ Go through the statements with the class, and explain that South Tyneside is a town in the north of England. Play the DVD for students to mark the sentences.

ANSWERS:
1 F (They think it's almost as important as numeracy and literacy.)
2 T
3 F (The first project was in Philadelphia.)
4 T
5 F (But he thinks they're better people for it.)

4a Students compare answers in pairs, then check with the class. Students then discuss the questions and see what they can remember.

b Students watch again and check answers before checking with the whole class.

ANSWERS:
1 the local authority
2 It was part of a psychology research programme.
3 do five kind things
4 The kids are better, deeper people.

5   If you have a multilingual class, then try to put students into groups of mixed nationality to discuss the questions. When they are ready, nominate students from each group to report back and find out if any other students have similar ideas.

World view (PAGE 65)

6a ⏵ Give students a minute to read through the statements first so they know what to listen for. Play the DVD for students to answer.

b Students compare in pairs, and see what they can remember about the false sentences. Encourage them to make notes.

7   Play the DVD again for students to add to their notes on the false statements. In feedback, nominate different students to summarise what the speakers said.

ANSWERS:
1 F (He thinks that people are happier now that everything is easier.)
2 T
3 T
4 F (She says that because people's basic needs are met, they look for other things to make them happy.)
5 T
6 F (They make people aspire to / want unnecessary things.)
7 T (She thinks it's a lofty ambition (= unrealistic).)
8 F (She thinks both are important. It should start with the parents, but then children spend a lot of time at school, so it's the teacher's responsibility there.)
9 T

8   Put students into groups to discuss the questions. When they have finished, nominate a student from each group to share their ideas with the class.

Find out more ⧉ (PAGE 65)

9   Students can either do this alone or in groups, depending on how big your class is. If you think students are likely to all choose the same option, then you might want to allocate the topic areas to different students in order to ensure a range of topics are covered. Students research their topic online, using the search terms provided, and make notes. Circulate and help with vocabulary where necessary.

Present your research

10 Go through the prompts, eliciting possible endings, and read the Tip with the class. Give students plenty of time to prepare their presentations, and help with vocabulary where necessary. When they are ready, students take turns presenting their findings. Encourage other students to listen and make notes, so that they can ask questions at the end of each presentation.

Students can now do Progress Test 3 on the Teacher's Resource Disc.

Grammar practice (PAGES 134–135)

See *Teaching tips: Using the Grammar and Vocabulary practice sections*, page 25.

Passive forms

ANSWERS:

1

1 could have been killed   2 ~~was~~ disappeared   3 love being given
4 ~~was~~ crashed   5 should be told   6 of being called
7 ~~was~~ happened   8 it's written

2

1 Audrey Hepburn was a British actress and humanitarian. She is best known as a film actor, and she received several awards for her roles. From the mid-1960s, she devoted more and more of her time to working with disadvantaged people through UNICEF, right up until her death in 1993.

2 Bali is a province of Indonesia, which covers the island of Bali and a few small neighbouring islands. It is nicknamed the 'Island of the Gods'. It is very popular with tourists and it is known for its highly developed arts. It is bordered by Java and Lombok to the west and east.

3 George R. R. Martin is an American fantasy author and screenwriter. He is best known for *A Song of Ice and Fire*, adapted for TV as *Game of Thrones*. He has written more than 20 books, as well as a number of screenplays.

4 The Eiffel Tower is a huge iron tower situated on the Champ de Mars in Paris. It was designed by engineers working for Gustave Eiffel's engineering company. It was erected in 1889 as the entrance to the World's Fair. It has had many uses since then, and during World War I the tower was used by the French military to communicate with ships in the Atlantic Ocean. Nowadays the tower is a popular tourist attraction, and it is visited by seven million people every year.

3

1 It is understood that the Princess is expecting her first baby.
The Princess is understood to be expecting her first baby.

2 It is expected that over 5,000 people will attend the music festival this weekend.
Over 5,000 people are expected to attend the music festival this weekend.

3 It is thought that Napoleon's recently discovered war diaries are fake.
Napoleon's recently discovered war diaries are thought to be fake.

4 It is alleged that the CEO embezzled funds in excess of $900,000.
The CEO is alleged to have embezzled funds in excess of $900,000.

5 It is reported that an anonymous telephone buyer paid over $20 million for the Dalí.
An anonymous telephone buyer is reported to have paid over $20 million for the Dalí.

6 It is rumoured that Johnny Depp is among the guests at the film festival.
Johnny Depp is rumoured to be among the guests at the film festival.

4

2 delivered   3 found   4 left   5 arrested   6 fined   7 named

5

b 7 – A baby born yesterday has been named Junior.com.
c 5 – A man wanted for armed robbery was arrested when he went to a police station to report his car being stolen.
d 6 – A woman fined $500 for riding her bicycle too fast has described the amount as unbelievable.
e 2 – A birthday card posted ten years ago has just arrived at its destination.
f 3 – Laboratory tests have confirmed that a finger found in a bag of popcorn was human.
g 4 – A piece of paper left at the scene of a crime had the robber's name and address on it.

6

1 Oh, sorry – I was told that Oscar Lopez worked here.
2 That customer shouldn't have been given a full refund.
3 Were you paid for all that extra work on the website you did?
4 I wish I had been taught how to drive when I was at school.
5 Although I was offered a better deal, I still decided to change phone company.
6 The wrong email was sent to hundreds of people because of a computer error.
7 In the event of a delay, passengers will be given a voucher for a free snack and drink.
8 What kind of questions were you asked at the interview?

7

1 *The suspect's girlfriend got arrested* means 'she was arrested'; *The suspect got his girlfriend arrested* means 'he caused her to be arrested'.
2 *restyle my hair* means 'I did it myself'; *have my hair restyled* means 'I paid someone else to do it'.
3 little difference in meaning – both sentences suggest it was an accident, although *I've got …* could imply 'it was my fault'.
4 *get your report finished* suggests it was difficult, whereas *finish your report* does not.
5 *got smashed* suggests it was accidental, whereas *were smashed* does not.
6 little difference in meaning – had + object + past participle is used to talk about something unpleasant that happened to us.

8

1 is known   2 is mainly produced   3 has been farmed   4 makes
5 lies   6 are selected   7 are then collected   8 be sold

Vocabulary practice (PAGE 157)
Education

ANSWERS:

1

1 numeracy   2 assessment   3 truancy   4 postgraduate
5 retake   6 scholarship   7 assignments   8 workshops

Learning

ANSWERS:

2

1 make   2 long-run   3 hang   4 build   5 put in   6 impact
7 shattered

Other words and phrases

ANSWERS:

3

1 sauntered off   2 're around   3 die down   4 see you off
5 speak out   6 eaten up

OVERVIEW

PAGES 66–67

Vocabulary and speaking: Descriptive adjectives

Common European Framework: Students can select an appropriate formulation from a broad range of language to express themselves clearly; can present clear, detailed descriptions on a wide range of subjects.

PAGES 68–69

Listening and vocabulary: Extreme fashion

Patterns to notice: Adding emphasis with auxiliaries and inversion

Pronunciation: Adding emphasis

Wordspot: *look*, *sound* and *feel*

Common European Framework: Students can understand interviews; can summarise and give their opinion about a discussion interview.

PAGES 70–71

Reading: There's no accounting for taste – *or is there?*

Grammar review: Adverbs

Common European Framework: Students can gather information from different parts of a text; can exchange, check and confirm accumulated factual information.

PAGES 72–73

Task: Rant or rave

Common European Framework: Students can give clear, detailed descriptions and presentations on complex subjects, developing particular points and rounding off with an appropriate conclusion.

PAGES 74–75

Writing: An online review

Speaking: Comment adverbials

Common European Framework: Students can write clear, detailed descriptions of real or imaginary events and experiences; can select an appropriate formulation from a broad range of language to express themselves clearly.

Vocabulary and speaking

(PAGES 66–67)

Descriptive adjectives

See *Teaching tips: Working with lexis*, page 21.

WARM UP

Introduce the topic by describing your bedroom when you were a teenager in as much detail as possible – try to include details such as the colour of the walls and furniture, any posters you had on the walls, etc. Give students a minute or two to sit on their own and try to visualise their bedroom when they were 12/13 years old. When they are ready, students describe their bedrooms to each other in pairs.

1 Focus the class on the photos and ask for their immediate reactions to one or two of them. Students could work in pairs to think of two adjectives for each picture, or this could be done as a whole class. Write their ideas on the board.

2a With weaker classes, you may want to go through the vocabulary first, checking understanding of each adjective before they match each group to a photo. Otherwise, students can work in pairs. In feedback, check that students understand and can pronounce: *twee* (too pretty or perfect, in a silly way), *vintage* /ˈvɪntɪdʒ/ (old, but high quality), *sleek* (smooth and attractive), *garish* (very brightly coloured and unpleasant), *frumpy* (unattractive and old-fashioned), *vulgar* /ˈvʌlgə/ (rude and offensive) and *scruffy* /ˈskrʌfi/ (dirty and untidy).

POSSIBLE ANSWERS:

1 D   2 H   3 B   4 C   5 F   6 G   7 A   8 E

b Students work in pairs before checking answers with the whole class.

ANSWERS:

Positive: cute, sweet, sleek, fun, sophisticated, chic, glamorous

Negative: twee, childish, outdated, stark, garish, frumpy, tacky, vulgar, over-the-top, scruffy, messy

Neutral: classic, vintage, minimal, contemporary, ultra-modern, colourful, outrageous, unconventional, provocative, conventional, casual

3 🎧 **7.1** Students listen and take notes then check in pairs. Play the recording again if necessary, then check answers with the class.

ANSWERS:

1 F – extravagant, unconventional, provocative, fun; positive
2 B – modern, slick, minimal; positive
3 G – attractive, frumpy, tacky, sophisticated, older; negative
4 E – clean-cut, scruffy, messy, refined, sophisticated, elegant; negative
5 C – abstract, broad, brash, garish; negative
6 H – classic, vintage; positive
7 D – hideous, twee, childish; negative
Photo A is not mentioned.

> **Vocabulary and speaking: Additional activity**
>
> To give students more practice in giving their opinions and using the vocabulary, bring/download a selection of pictures showing different styles from magazines and/or websites, for students to discuss. The pictures could be stuck around the classroom walls, and students walk around and share their opinions.

4a Start by doing one or two examples about yourself, then give students a few minutes to think about their answers. Check understanding/pronunciation of *navel* /ˈneɪvəl/ (small circle in the middle of your stomach), *loud* (unpleasantly bright), psychedelic /ˌsaɪkəˈdelɪk/ (bright, complicated pattern) and *fancy* (informal, negative connotation; too big, bright or expensive).

b Students compare answers in pairs. When they have finished, ask a few students to report back to the class.

> **Vocabulary and speaking, exercise 4: Alternative suggestion**
>
> If your students know each other quite well, instead of telling each other their answers to the questions, students can guess which of the things their partner would like to do, e.g. *'I think you would secretly like to get a tattoo.' 'Yes, you're right!'* You could demonstrate this first by asking students to make guesses about you.

ADDITIONAL PRACTICE

➡ **Resource bank:** Activity 7C *Guess the picture* (Descriptive adjectives)

Vocabulary practice: Exercise 1

Workbook: Vocabulary, *Descriptive adjectives*, page 34

Listening and vocabulary

(PAGES 68–69)

Extreme fashion

WARM UP

If you have any, then bring in any old clothes you have – the stranger the better – and show them to students. Alternatively, you could bring any photos you have of yourself when you were younger, especially if you wore any strange fashion choices. Ask if any students have worn similar strange clothes in the past.

1a Put students into groups to think of words, and set a strict time limit of two minutes. With stronger classes, you could ask them to add two or three words to each category. While they are doing it, copy the word web onto the board.

b Check answers with the class, awarding points and writing the words on the word web on the board.

2 Focus attention on the photos, and answer the question as a class.

> **ANSWERS:**
> **In the photos:** platform shoes, glasses with big frames, wig, corset
> **Word web:**
> 1 shoulder pads, corset
> 2 glasses with big frames, wig, ponytail
> 3 jumpsuit
> 4 leggings
> 5 platform shoes, ankle socks

3 Students discuss the questions in pairs. When they are ready, compare answers as a class.

> **POSSIBLE ANSWERS:**
> **from left to right:**
> **Photo 1** – question 1; **Photo 2** – questions 3 and 4;
> **Photo 3** – questions 2 and 5; **Photo 4** – questions 2 and 5;
> **Photo 5** – question 3

4 🎧 **7.2** Check understanding of *miscarriage* (losing a baby before it's born) and *catwalk* (long, raised area where models walk during a fashion show). Students listen and order the questions then check in pairs, before checking with the whole class. Elicit how much students can remember about each question.

> **ANSWERS:**
> A 5   B 2   C 4   D 1   E 3

5 🎧 **7.3** Give students a minute or two to read through the questions and guess the answers. When they are ready, play the recording for students to listen and check. Check answers with the class.

> **ANSWERS:**
> 1 c   2 b   3 b   4 c   5 b

6 Put students into groups to read the questions and choose which they want to discuss. In feedback, nominate students from each group to share their ideas with the class.

> **PATTERNS TO NOTICE**
>
> **Adding emphasis with auxiliaries and inversion**
> 1 Write the examples on the board and elicit how the auxiliaries are used to add emphasis. Drill the sentences with the class.
>
> > **ANSWERS:**
> > 1 I do think some of the stories told about them are in fact exaggerated.
> > 2 That really did happen!
>
> **2 & 3** Go through the explanations with the class and elicit one or two further examples.

7 Read the example with the class. Students work alone then check in pairs, before checking answers with the whole class.

8 🎧 **7.4** Play the recording, pausing after each sentence for students to practise saying the sentences.

> **ANSWERS:**
> 2 I felt <u>really</u> sorry for Charlie when I saw him yesterday.
> 3 This flat is a mess. I <u>do</u> think you have a responsibility to help with the housework.
> 4 I'm absolutely exhausted! I <u>really</u> need to get some sleep!
> 5 I'm sorry, but the way Gina behaves <u>does</u> annoy me.
> 6 I know you think I don't like your cooking, but I <u>do</u> like it.
> 7 I was <u>definitely</u> relieved when the day was over!

> **Pronunciation, exercise 8: Additional suggestion**
>
> To give students practice of the emphasis patterns in conversation, put them into pairs and ask them to extend one or two of the examples in exercise 7 into four to six line conversations. Once students have prepared their conversations, they can act them out for the class.

ADDITIONAL PRACTICE

➡ **Resource bank:** Activity 7B *Name that thing!* (Adding emphasis with auxiliaries and inversion)

Workbook: Vocabulary: *Extreme fashion*, page 34; Grammar: *Adding emphasis with auxiliaries and inversion*, page 35; Pronunciation: *Emphasis with auxiliaries and inversion*, page 35;

Wordspot (PAGE 69)

look, *sound* and *feel*

See *Teaching tips: Working with lexis*, page 21.

1a With stronger classes, you could lead in by asking students for some examples of these words as verbs and nouns, in sentences, e.g. *You look fantastic. / Lady Gaga's got a new look.*; *This song sounds familiar. / There's a strange sound coming from the other room.* Explain that there are a lot of idioms, compound nouns, etc. which use these words, and put students into pairs to do exercise 1a.

> **ANSWERS:**
> 1 a lookalike   2 dirty   3 up to   4 bite   5 off   6 effects
> 7 soundtrack   8 feel-good   9 on top of the world   10 mixed

Notes on vocabulary

A *lookout* is someone who watches carefully to warn other people of danger, e.g. *Johnny, who was the lookout, shouted that someone was coming.*

An *onlooker* is someone who watches something without being involved, e.g. *A crowd of onlookers waited to see who would get out of the black limousine.*

b Focus attention on the cartoons and answer the question as a class.

ANSWERS:

left: feeling on top of the world

right: give someone a dirty look

2 🎧 **7.5** Play the recording, stopping after the first example to check that students understand what to do. Check answers as a class. Students could then read the audio script to look more closely at how the phrases were used.

ANSWERS:

1 sound	2 Feel	3 look	4 sound	5 sound	6 look
7 Look	8 feel	9 sound	10 feel	11 look	12 feelings

3 🎧 **7.6** You could play the first couple of questions as examples, demonstrating how to write the answers in random order on the board. Stop the recording as necessary, to give students time to think and write. Students can either work in pairs and swap papers with their partner, or walk around the class and talk to different people about their answers.

ADDITIONAL PRACTICE

➡ **Resource bank:** Activity 7D *How does it feel?* (*look*, *sound* and *feel*)

Vocabulary practice: Exercise 2

Workbook: Wordspot: *look*, *sound* and *feel*, page 35

Reading (PAGES 70–71)

There's no accounting for taste – or is there?

1 You could introduce the topic by telling students about your own tastes in some of the areas. Students then discuss the questions in pairs. When they are ready, ask students to share their ideas with the class and find out if any students have similar tastes in common.

2 Make sure students only read the introduction and the headings, and not the article at this stage. Elicit students' predictions and write them on the board.

3a Explain that students will have to retell what they've read, and they can take notes to help if they want. While they're reading, be on hand to help with comprehension and/or any new vocabulary.

b Encourage students to ask follow-up questions and ask for clarification while they listen.

4 Answer the question as a class, nominating students to give their opinions.

5 Give students enough time to read the rest of the article and answer the questions. Check answers as a class.

ANSWERS:

1 They were able to disguise their real Scottish accents, and convince talent spotters that they had a real west-coast American style.
2 They were heartbroken and went back to Scotland feeling very disappointed.
3 Because he was unable to sell enough paintings during his lifetime.
4 At a restaurant on the second floor of the Eiffel Tower. It was the one place in Paris where he couldn't see the tower.
5 Because he proved that people would not like expensive wine if they thought it was cheap.
6 Because the price was doubled. Customers were more interested in buying something expensive.

6 Focus attention on the quotes and check understanding. Students discuss in pairs before discussing as a class.

ADDITIONAL PRACTICE

➡ **Workbook:** Listen and read: *An extract from a biography*, page 36

Grammar review (PAGE 71)
Adverbs

See *Teaching tips: Using a discovery approach to grammar*, page 20.

1 With weaker classes, you could ask them to reread the section on adverbs in the Language summary for Unit 4 on page 125 before they start. Start by eliciting one or two types of adverbs, e.g. of frequency (*sometimes*, *usually*), manner (*sadly*, *quickly*), degree (*very*, *really*), etc. Students work in pairs, then check answers with the class.

ANSWERS:

2 So what was the difference? **Amazingly**, it was their accent.
3 Their Scottish accents hadn't gone down **well**.
4 'They **just** laughed at us,' recalled Gavin.
5 **At that time**, everyone expected rappers to be American.
6 Some people are **simply** ahead of their time.
7 When plans for the Eiffel Tower were first proposed, Parisians protested **loudly**.
8 When the tower **finally** opened, everyone changed their mind.
9 Maupassant **frequently** ate dinner in the tower's second floor restaurant.
10 The range of products on offer can be **completely** bewildering.
11 We **often** look to price as an indication of quality.

2 Students work in pairs then check answers with the class.

ANSWERS:

a even, just   **b** at that time, finally   **c** well, loudly
d frequently, often   **e** amazingly, simply   **f** completely
g go down well, protest loudly, completely bewildering

You may want to ask students to read Language summary 7 on pages 136–137 for a more detailed explanation of adverbs.

3 Give students a few minutes to change the sentences, then compare answers in pairs. In feedback, ask a few students to report back to the class.

ANSWERS:

1 really hard   2 hardly ever   3 really well   4 even
5 for ten years   6 really

ADDITIONAL PRACTICE

➡ **Resource bank:** Activity 7A *Advertise it!* (Adverbs)

Grammar practice: Exercises 1–9

Workbook: Grammar: *Adverbs*, pages 37–38

Task (PAGES 72–73)
Rant or rave

See *Teaching tips: Making tasks work*, page 23.

WARM UP

Introduce the topic by telling students about one or two of your own pet hates (e.g. people who walk slowly in front of you, people who take up more than one seat on a train/bus, etc.). Ask students if they agree and have any similar pet hates.

Preparation (PAGE 72)
Listening

1a Focus attention on the words/phrases and elicit the first one or two as an example. Students discuss whether the rest refer to positive or negative feelings in pairs, before checking answers with the whole class. Check pronunciation of *spectacular* /spek'tækjələ/, *awesome* /'ɔːsəm/, *monstrosity* /mɒn'strɒsɪti/, *gross* /grəʊs/ and *tedious* /'tiːdɪəs/.

ANSWERS:

positive: just took my breath away, absolutely spectacular, awesome, just magic, genius

negative: fundamentally immoral, a monstrosity, it drives me mad, disgusting, a real creep, totally gross, a waste of time, tedious

b Students discuss in pairs before comparing ideas with the whole class.

2 🎧 7.7 Students listen and answer the questions, then check in pairs. Play the recording again if necessary, before checking answers with the whole class. In feedback, ask students if they agree or disagree with the speakers.

ANSWERS:

Speaker 1: hip-hop music (a style of music): she loves it, it's cool, it can be poetic, and rappers are verbal geniuses

Speaker 2: football referees (a type of behaviour): he hates corruption in the game

Speaker 3: the royal family (something you hate that everyone else seems to love): it's immoral that they have so much wealth when poor people can't afford to heat their homes

Speaker 4: going to the theatre (an activity): it's a type of magic to see people acting in front of you

Speaker 5: social media (something you hate that everyone else seems to love): he doesn't like people sharing lots of details about their lives

3 Go through the phrases in the Useful language box, eliciting possible endings for each one. Students listen again and tick the phrases they hear. Check answers with the class.

ANSWERS:

Speaker 2: I think ... to be honest ...

Speaker 3: There's one thing that really gets on my nerves ... , It makes me absolutely furious!, It seems very odd to me that ...

Speaker 4: There's nothing like it.

Preparation: Alternative suggestions

Instead of using the recording:

a Provide the model yourself. Think of two or three things you love/hate and prepare a few notes to speak from, covering your main reasons for loving/hating the things you are talking about, but do not read from a script. Try to incorporate one or two of the words/phrases from exercise 1 and some of the Useful language, so that students can tick off the phrases they hear you use while you are 'ranting/raving'. It would also be a good idea to bring in some pictures of your pet hates (e.g. a politician, a singer, a building, etc.), or the thing itself (e.g. a song, an item of clothing, a type of food, etc.), to 'support' your rant or rave.

b Ask someone you know, e.g. another teacher in the school, to come in and talk about something they love or hate. Give them the words/phrases in exercise 1 and the Useful language to select from and ask them to speak from notes rather than reading a script. Suggest that they bring in pictures or the thing itself to show the students.

Task (PAGES 72–73)
Speaking

1 Give students plenty of time to think about and choose their topics. Go around and help with ideas and vocabulary, writing any new words/phrases on the board.

2 Students compare their choices in pairs, and see if they have any ideas in common.

3a Remind students of the Useful language box, and ask students to take it in turns to rant/rave to the class. Ask other students to think about whether they agree/disagree and why.

b Hold a class vote via a show of hands.

Task: Alternative suggestions

If you feel some students will be shy or embarrassed about 'ranting':

a They may feel more comfortable taking on the role of someone else, e.g. a famous politician, film star, etc. and preparing to rant 'in character' about things they think that person would hate.

b Ask them to rant/rave in pairs. When they have finished, ask a few students to report back to the class.

Follow up (PAGE 73)
Writing

1 When students have written their comments, display them around the class. Ask other students to walk around and read them, and write their own comments underneath. Alternatively, if you have a class web page or social networking page, you could set up forum threads to discuss each topic online and encourage each student to add their comments.

Share your task

Some additional ideas could include:

- Students film/record their rants/raves. Other students watch/listen then vote which rave to keep and which rant to 'banish'.
- Students film/record themselves without saying what it is they're ranting/raving about. Other students watch/listen and guess what it is.
- Students act out a situation described in their rant or rave.

Language live (PAGES 74–75)

Writing (PAGE 74)

An online review

WARM UP

Print or show some online reviews for different things, e.g. products from shopping websites, restaurants/hotels from tourist websites, etc. Ask students to read through them quickly to decide if each one is a good or bad review, then underline any new words/phrases.

1 To introduce the topic, you could show one or two online review sites and/or tell students about what you use online reviews for (e.g. when buying things online, films, etc.). Discuss the questions as a class.

2 Students read the review and order the points, then check in pairs. Check answers with the class.

ANSWERS:

location – the positives – the negatives – overall opinion

3a Write *great* on the board and elicit other ways of saying it, with more impact (e.g. *amazing*, *superb*, etc.). Students discuss alternatives to the other words in pairs.

b Students replace the words in bold in pairs. Check answers with the class, and ask if anyone came up with the same words/phrases in exercise 3a.

ANSWERS:

great – impressive / its big selling point
close to – within easy walking distance of
good – positive
OK – perfectly adequate
very nice – impressive / its big selling point
not good – disappointing, to say the least / fails to impress
done more – gone out of their way
not great – disappointing, to say the least / fails to impress

4 Focus attention on review B and elicit what it's for. Students read and classify the phrases alone then check in pairs. Check answers with the class, and answer any questions students have about the vocabulary.

ANSWERS:

Positive: thought-provoking, leaves a lasting impression, on the edge of our seats, gripping and believable, breathtaking, mesmerising, a refreshing lack of, not to be missed
Negative: clunky, isn't quite up to the same high standards, slightly wide of the mark, a few too many

5a Students work alone then check in pairs, before checking answers with the whole class.

POSSIBLE ANSWERS:

1 breathtaking   2 up to the same high standards
3 impressive   4 big selling point   5 fails to impress
6 isn't quite up to the same high standards   7 perfectly adequate
8 clunky   9 a few too many   10 not to be missed

b Students work in pairs. In feedback, write the words on the board and check understanding.

POSSIBLE ANSWERS:

filler tracks, unmistakeable voice, raw talent and eclectic style, lyrics, chorus, standout albums

6a Refer students back to the order of points covered in exercise 2 to help structure their reviews. Go around and help with ideas and vocabulary, writing any new words/phrases on the board.

b Give students time to check their reviews and swap with a partner to check. Students can either write the final draft in class or for homework.

Speaking (PAGE 75)

Comment adverbials

1 Do one or two examples with the class, then put them into pairs to do the rest.

ANSWERS:

a I'm glad to say, Thank goodness, It's a good job
b To be perfectly honest, Quite frankly, To tell the truth
c to make matters worse, I'm afraid to say
d All being well
e Amazingly enough, Much to my surprise, Funnily enough, To my utter astonishment

2 🎧 7.8 Students read through the question before they listen to the two reviews. Students check answers in pairs before checking with the whole class.

ANSWERS:

Review 1: a new TV: doesn't like the hand-waving system; likes the image and sound quality

Review 2: a pair of jeans: doesn't like them because the pockets are small, the dye in the denim comes off easily and the buttons fall off

3 Students can discuss this in pairs, then listen again to check. You may want to stop the recording after each phrase, so that students can copy the pronunciation, particularly the way that the speaker pauses briefly after the comment adverbial.

ANSWERS:

1 Now, amazingly enough
2 to be perfectly honest
3 I'm glad to say
4 all being well
5 to tell the truth
6 Quite frankly
7 thank goodness
8 much to my surprise
9 It's a good job
10 To make matters worse
11 Funnily enough
12 To my utter astonishment

4a–b Elicit students' ideas as to what they could write about and write them on the board. Give students time to write their scripts and go around helping with vocabulary, encouraging them to use the comment adverbials from exercise 1. When they are ready, ask students to read out their reviews to the class.

ADDITIONAL PRACTICE

➡ **Workbook:** Writing: *An online review*, page 38; Language live: *Comment adverbials*, page 38

Grammar practice (PAGES 138–139)

See *Teaching tips: Using the Grammar and Vocabulary practice sections*, page 25.

Adverbs

ANSWERS:

1

1 Still   2 already   3 already   4 still   5 yet   6 already
7 still   8 yet

2

1 We hope to come back here very soon.
2 James (quickly) read the text message (quickly) then (carefully) put his phone down (carefully).
3 Let's all get together for coffee sometime.
4 Could you possibly give me a hand with this shopping?
5 Briggs played really well all afternoon yesterday.
6 The air conditioning comes on automatically in all the rooms at six o'clock every morning / every morning at six o'clock.
7 Did you see anyone in the car park just now?

5

1 This **simple** little pasta dish is quick and easy to prepare, but the ingredients complement each other so **perfectly** that you'll love every bite!
2 Bring a **heavy** pan of water to the boil, then cook half a kilo of **fresh** pasta for about three minutes, or until it floats. Drain and set aside.
3 **Roughly** chop half an onion and crush two cloves of garlic, and fry them in a little olive oil until **(slightly)** soft and **(slightly)** brown.
4 Meanwhile, slice a courgette **finely** and add that to the onion and garlic, and cook for another five minutes, stirring **continuously**.
5 Turn the heat off and add the pasta and 150g parmesan cheese, then **(quickly)** mix everything together **(quickly)** before the cheese melts too much.
6 Slice two lemons and **(generously)** squeeze the juice over the pasta **(generously)**, then mix everything together.
7 Season with a little salt and **freshly** ground black pepper.
8 Tastes **great** with ciabatta and a **dry** white wine.

6

1 deeply   2 hardly   3 wrong   4 free   5 late   6 rightly

7

1 club together   2 tried desperately   3 understand perfectly
4 feel strongly   5 eating sensibly   6 complained bitterly
7 apologise(d) profusely   8 sold ... well   9 reacts ... badly
10 went ... smoothly

8

1 Friends are made by many acts – and lost by **only** one.
2 It is **only** the intellectually lost who ever argue.
3 Nothing is **particularly** hard if you divide it into small jobs.
4 It takes **especially** good manners to put up with bad ones.
5 It is **even** easier to forgive an enemy than to forgive a friend.
6 If a wife **always** laughs at her husband's jokes, is he funny or is she smart?
7 **Only** a brilliant man knows whether the applause for his words is politeness or appreciation.
8 Silence is **often** misinterpreted, but **never** misquoted.
9 **Never** answer a letter while you are angry.
10 I don't **even** know anything about music. In my line, you don't have to.

Sentences 1, 2, 4, 5, 7 and 10 use focusing adverbs (*only, even, especially*).

9

1 It smells ~~nicely~~ **nice**.
2 She's been working really ~~hardly~~ **hard**.
3 we have ~~already~~ **yet** to see
4 it's ~~greatly~~ **highly** unlikely the new product
5 It looks really ~~well~~ **good** on you.
6 ~~Even~~ **Only** a few people turned up.
7 the people felt very ~~deep~~ **deeply**
8 when Vinnie arrived ~~lately~~ **late** for class
9 **On the way home**, we stopped off
10 I try to do ~~as often~~ exercise **as often** as I can.

Vocabulary practice (PAGE 158)

Descriptive adjectives

ANSWERS:

1

1 twee   2 stark   3 sleek   4 garish   5 frumpy   6 tacky
7 vulgar   8 scruffy

look, sound and *feel*

ANSWERS:

2

1 sound   2 feelings   3 look   4 look   5 sound   6 feel

Other words and phrases

ANSWERS:

3

1 instant hit   2 went down   3 living the dream
4 the benefit of hindsight   5 heartbroken

OVERVIEW

PAGES 76–77

Vocabulary and speaking: Characteristics and behaviour

Patterns to notice: Describing typical habits

Common European Framework: Students can express themselves fluently and spontaneously without much obvious searching for expressions; can use language flexibly and effectively.

PAGES 78–79

Listening: Leaving home

Grammar review: Infinitives and *-ing* forms

Wordspot: *just*

Common European Framework: Students can understand extended speech even when it is not clearly structured; can express themselves clearly on a wide range of topics.

PAGES 80–81

Reading: A bluffer's guide to men and women

Patterns to notice: Compound phrases: *a lack of …, a tendency to …,* etc.

Common European Framework: Students can scan quickly through long and complex texts, locating relevant details; can explain a viewpoint on a topical issue.

PAGES 82–83

Task: Choose celebrities for a charity trek

Common European Framework: Students can express their ideas and opinions with precision, present and respond to complex lines of argument convincingly.

PAGES 84–85

World culture: Running a large family

Common European Framework: Students can identify speaker viewpoints and attitudes as well as the information content; can give a clear, systematically developed presentation, with highlighting of significant points, and relevant supporting detail.

Vocabulary and speaking

(PAGES 76–77)

Characteristics and behaviour

See *Teaching tips: Working with lexis*, page 21.

WARM UP

Write the following on the board: *pay bills, clean the house, wash the clothes, do repairs, cook, do the shopping, wash the dishes.* Students discuss who does each of these things in the place where they live in small groups. In feedback, nominate a student from each group to share their ideas with the class.

1a Focus attention on the list and check understanding of the types of households, using the photos. Put students into groups to discuss the questions.

b Establish what reasons people have for living away from their family, e.g. when they move to a different place to study or to work. Put students into groups to discuss the questions.

POSSIBLE ANSWERS:

Advantages of living away from the family: more independence and freedom, more people of your own age to be friends with

Disadvantages: more responsibility, bills to pay, missing your family

2a Students work on the descriptions individually or in pairs. Encourage them to try to work out the meaning of any unfamiliar vocabulary from the context, and only use a dictionary / mobile phone to check those they are really unsure of. Check pronunciation of *irritable* /ˈɪrɪtəbəl/, *laid-back* /ˈleɪdˈbæk/, *overbearing* /əʊvəˈbeərɪŋ/ (always trying to control other people) and *unwind* /ʌnˈwaɪnd/ (relax).

b Students discuss the characteristics in small groups. Ideas for other behaviour which is difficult to live with: *mean with money and always querying their share of the bills, very bossy and telling everyone else in the house what to do, playing loud music*, etc.

3a 🎧 **8.1** Establish that the people could be talking about a family member, or a friend/flatmate/roommate. Students listen then check answers in pairs.

b Students listen again and make notes. In feedback, nominate students to summarise what they heard.

ANSWERS:

Speaker 1: her sister (she sulks, and doesn't say what the problem is)

Speaker 2: her roommate (she is a chatterbox, and always wants to talk about what happens to her)

Speaker 3: an ex-flatmate (he was unpredictable and changed moods a lot)

Speaker 4: her boyfriend (he's opinionated and doesn't really listen)

Speaker 5: her ex-husband (he was a neat freak and was very fussy about putting things in the right place)

4 Give students a few minutes to prepare what they are going to say, then put them into pairs to tell each other. Afterwards, you could ask one or two pairs to report back to the class on anything they found in common.

PATTERNS TO NOTICE

Describing typical habits

1–3 Write the following examples of present habits on the board, and ask students how to make these into past habits:

She'll go off in a corner and sulk.

She won't pick up the phone.

She's always laughing.

He's always moaning.

Then give students a few minutes to read through the examples in the box.

Notes on past habits

Check that students understand the following:

– all the patterns here can be used to describe good or bad typical behaviour

– *will* is used here to talk about the present, not the future

– *always* is used with the Present or Past continuous (rather than the Present or Past simple) to emphasise how frequently the habit is repeated – other adverbs commonly used are *constantly* and *forever*

– *would* is used here to talk about the past, it is not part of a hypothetical sentence

– *used to go* could be replaced with *would go* without changing the meaning

– *on* after *keep* emphasises the frequency of the action

– *keep* + *-ing* describes a repeated action, whereas *tend to* can describe an action or a state

---

ADDITIONAL PRACTICE

Resource bank: Activity 8B *That's just typical!* (Describing typical habits); Activity 8C *You're so ...* (Characteristics and behaviour)

Vocabulary practice: Exercise 1

Workbook: Vocabulary: *Characteristics and behaviour*, page 39; Grammar: *Describing typical habits*, page 39

Listening (PAGE 78)

Leaving home

1a–b Put students into groups to discuss the questions, then report back to the class on common reasons they thought of for leaving home.

2a Give students a few minutes to read about the three people.

> **ANSWERS:**
> **Peter:** left to join the army
> **Liz:** left to go to boarding school
> **Catherine:** left to work in France

b Students can work in pairs to predict who will mention each topic, and make notes in pencil in the first column.

3a 🎧 **8.2** Students listen to check their predictions and make notes in the second column.

> **ANSWERS:**
> **1** Peter **2** Peter **3** Liz **4** Catherine **5** Catherine
> **6** Catherine **7** Peter **8** Peter **9** Liz

b Students listen again and note as much information as they can, before checking answers in pairs. In feedback, ask students to tell you as much information as they can.

> **ANSWERS:**
> **1** He was really looking forward to it.
> **2** These were the first things they taught him in the army.
> **3** It was a wonderfully free life.
> **4** She'd go to the beach every day.
> **5** The children didn't really want to do it, so it was hard work getting them to sit down at the table and study.
> **6** She didn't like it, but after a while got used to it.
> **7** They had their hair cut off on the second day, and another boy who had looked tough suddenly looked very small.
> **8** He did, but that was the point – they needed to be able to act as a unit.
> **9** Because she had to work so hard, she got used to it and it made her more independent as a person.

4 Put students into small groups to discuss the questions, encouraging them to give reasons for their opinions as much as possible. Ask one or two groups to report back to the class.

Grammar review (PAGE 79)

Infinitives and *-ing* forms

See *Teaching tips: Using a discovery approach to grammar*, page 20.

1a–b Students try to remember who said each phrase in pairs, before checking answers with the audio script.

> **ANSWERS:**
> **1** Peter **2** Liz **3** Catherine **4** Catherine **5** Catherine
> **6** Catherine **7** Catherine **8** Peter **9** Liz **10** Liz

2 Put students into pairs to find the examples. You could suggest that student A looks for a–d, while student B looks for e–i, then they exchange the examples they have found. Circulate and help as required.

> **ANSWERS:**
> **a** 5, 6 **b** 2, 7, 9, 10 **c** 5, 6, 10 **d** 5 **e** 3 **f** 4 **g** 1
> **h** 8 **i** 7

3 Students discuss the differences in pairs. Check answers with the class, going through the points in the answer key and giving further examples where necessary.

> **ANSWERS:**
> **1** *stopped to have* = stop what you are doing to do something else
> *stopped having* = stop completely, quit
> **2** *trying to open* = attempting to do something
> *try opening* = experiment with something to see if it works
> **3** *remember to tell* = not forget to do something in the future
> *remember telling* = have a memory of something in the past

You may want to ask students to read Language summary 8 on pages 140–141 for a more detailed explanation of infinitives and *-ing* forms.

4 Do one or two examples of your own, then give students a minute or two to complete the sentences. They can compare answers in small groups, or walk around the class and compare with others.

> **Grammar review, exercise 4: Alternative suggestion**
> When they have completed the sentences, put students into small groups. Students take it in turns to read out only their endings, while other students listen and guess which sentence it completes.

ADDITIONAL PRACTICE

Resource bank: Activity 8A *Verb cards* (Infinitives and *-ing* forms)

Grammar practice: Exercises 1–9

Workbook: Grammar: *Infinitives and* -ing *forms*, pages 40–42

Wordspot (PAGE 79)

just

See *Teaching tips: Working with lexis*, page 21.

WARM UP

Write *just* on the board and ask students what it means. Elicit a few different meanings/uses and example sentences, and write them on the board. At the end of exercise 1, revisit the sentences on the board and elicit where they go in the word web.

1 Focus students on the word web and go through the examples of the different meanings of *just*. Students work individually or in pairs to decide which meanings are used in the sentences. With stronger classes, you could ask them to think of another example for each category.

> **ANSWERS:**
>
> **b** 2   **c** 3   **d** 1   **e** 4   **f** 3   **g** 1   **h** 3   **i** 5   **j** 3

2 Do the first example with the class, then students can work in pairs on the rest.

3 🎧 **8.3** Play the recording for students to compare their answers. In feedback, check answers and ask if students had any different answers.

> **POSSIBLE ANSWERS:**
>
> 1 I'll just take your coat for you. (polite phrase)
> 2 I was so annoyed, I just tore up the letter and walked out. (for emphasis)
> 3 I'm just looking, thank you. ('only')
> 4 The weather was just perfect for my birthday party. (for emphasis)
> 5 These shoes are just what I need. ('exactly')
> 6 I'll just be a few minutes and then we can go. ('only')
> 7 Look! I've just found that receipt you were looking for. (a short time before)
> 8 Lunch is just a sandwich. I hope that's OK. ('only')
> 9 Would you mind just holding this for me, please? (polite phrase)
> 10 I've got just enough money to pay! ('only')

4 Students ask and answer in pairs.

ADDITIONAL PRACTICE

➡ **Resource bank:** Activity 8D *Just the phrase* (*just*)
Vocabulary practice: Exercises 2a–b
Workbook: Wordspot: *just*, page 42

Reading (PAGES 80–81)

A bluffer's guide to men and women

WARM UP

Write the following jobs on the board: *fire fighter*, *pilot*, *shop assistant*, *teacher*, *nurse*, *receptionist*, *soldier*. In pairs, students discuss which of the jobs have traditionally been done by men and which by women (and which by both) in their country/ies, and if the same is still true today.

1 Note that these quotations set the tone for the reading text which follows – light-hearted and not to be taken too seriously. With weaker classes, you may need to explain the following: *to marry beneath you* means to marry someone who is socially inferior and the word *finished* can have different meanings – either 'completed' or 'ended, no longer able to function properly'. Give students a few minutes to read and discuss the one(s) they liked best/least, either with a partner or as a class.

2a–b Give students a few minutes to consider their answers, before comparing ideas in small groups.

3a Explain that a 'Bluffer's guide' is usually written for people who know very little about a subject, but want to pretend they know a lot and therefore need to pick up 'key' facts quickly. Establish that the extracts from the two books have been mixed up, so students have to decide if each extract is about men or women. Complete the first extract as an example, then give them time to read and complete the rest. Students compare answers in pairs or small groups, before checking answers on page 108.

b Refer students back to the characteristics in exercise 2a and ask them to compare their answers to those in the text.

> **ANSWERS:**
>
> a tendency to be competitive: men
> an ability to ignore mess: men
> a desire for approval: women
> a tendency to nag: women
> an inability to make decisions: men
> a tendency to feel guilty: women
> a fear of commitment: men
> a need for attention: women

4a–b Give students a few minutes to think about their answers, then put them into small groups to discuss the questions.

> **PATTERNS TO NOTICE**
>
> **Compound phrases:** *a lack of ...*, *a tendency to ...*, etc.
>
> 1 Go through the notes with the class, then give students a few minutes to find further examples in exercise 2a in pairs.
>
> > **ANSWERS:**
> >
> > a a lack of self-confidence, a desire for approval, a love of gadgets, a fear of failure, a sense of superiority, a fear of commitment, a need for attention
> > b a tendency to be, an ability to ignore, a tendency to nag, an inability to make, a tendency to feel
>
> 2 Go through the examples with the class, and elicit possible adjectives that could be used with the examples in 1 (e.g. *a complete lack of self-confidence, a slight tendency to be competitive*, etc.)

> **Patterns to notice: Alternative suggestion**
>
> Give students the opportunity to work out some of the patterns in the box by writing the phrases on slips of paper, e.g.
>
> *fear of failure*
> *lack of self-confidence*
> *need for approval*
> *a tendency to panic*
>
> Give each pair or group a set of slips to try to put into groups. As you go through the answers, ask students for more examples of nouns or infinitives that could fit into the pattern (e.g. *fear of rejection*). Finally, direct students to the examples in the box.
>
> As you go through the examples in the box, you could ask students whether each phrase describes a positive or negative characteristic.

5a 🎧 **8.4** Play the recording, pausing after each phrase for students to write their answers.

> **ANSWERS:**
> **2** a big fear of rejection **3** a love of adventure
> **4** a tendency to worry **5** a constant need to show off
> **6** an enormous desire to please **7** an amazing lack of ambition
> **8** a great sense of fun **9** this need for reassurance
> **10** this strange ability to read your mind
> **11** a weird sense of achievement
> **12** a complete inability to see other people's point of view

b 🎧 **8.5** Play the recording, pausing after each phrase for students to repeat. Make sure they are linking the words smoothly.

6a Focus students on the example and ask them to think of one more. Give them time to work individually on the rest of the answers.

b Students compare answers in groups or walk around the class, comparing with others.

ADDITIONAL PRACTICE

➡ **Workbook:** Listen and read: *Daggers drawn*, pages 42–43; Grammar: *Compound phrases*, page 42; Pronunciation: *Stress in compound phrases*, page 43

Task (PAGES 82–83)

Choose celebrities for a charity trek

See *Teaching tips: Making tasks work*, page 23.

WARM UP

Prepare information on three different charities, with different aims, by downloading or writing a short description of each, or directing students to their websites. Ask students to look through / read the information, then discuss which they like best and why.

Preparation (PAGES 82–83)

Reading

1 Focus attention on the photos and the title and elicit students' ideas as to what the task is about. Students read the text then summarise the points in pairs. In feedback, nominate different pairs to summarise each of the points to the class.

> **ANSWERS:**
> Operation Educate aims to provide buildings and equipment to schools in poor areas around the world.
> The safari trek aims to raise money and increase the charity's public profile and status. Six celebrities will go from the north to the south of Africa in a 4x4 and it will be on daytime TV.
> The celebrities need to be able to drive, navigate and film themselves, be able to keep going and work as a team. The ones who climb Kilimanjaro also need to be very fit.
> The organising committee also need to decide which celebrities will go, a reserve in case of a drop-out, who will be the media spokesperson, who will be the group leader and which three will climb Kilimanjaro.

2a Refer students to the profiles on pages 110–111. Students underline key factors and circle the negative points then compare in pairs.

b Students discuss the questions in pairs.

Task (PAGES 82–83)

Speaking

1 Students decide on six candidates in groups, then make notes to justify their decisions. Circulate and help with vocabulary as required.

2 Put students into new groups to agree on the best six candidates. Focus attention on the Useful language box, sections a and b and elicit possible ways of ending each phrase. Monitor and note down examples of good language use and/or errors for feedback and correction later.

> **Task, exercise 2: Additional suggestion**
> Provide students with a model of the task by recording yourself and two or three other people (e.g. teachers in the school) discussing and agreeing on six candidates. Do not script the discussion, but do try to incorporate some of the Useful language. Students listen and compare your choices with theirs, and analyse the language you used by ticking off any phrases they hear from the Useful language box, and by making a note of other phrases.

3 Refer students to the Useful language box, sections c and d. Each group member could present one or two candidates to the class, depending on how many people are in the group. While they do this, you could write up the six names chosen by each group, so that the class can compare the choices afterwards and see which candidates everyone agreed on. Encourage the groups to try to persuade others to change their minds, so that the whole class ends up with the same six names.

> **Share your task**
> Some additional ideas could include:
> - Students film/record the task as a 'press conference', with other students taking the role of journalists and asking and answering questions.
> - Students take the roles of the celebrities on pages 110–111 of the Students' Book and film/record a short talk on why they should be chosen.
> - Students film/record themselves acting out one of the 'challenges' from the trip.
> - Students film/record themselves acting out interviews with successful and unsuccessful celebrities.

ADDITIONAL PRACTICE

➡ **Workbook:** Writing: *An announcement*, page 43

World culture (PAGES 84–85)

Running a large family

> **Culture notes**
> In the US in 1800, the average number of children per family was seven. By 1900, this had halved to 3.5. At the same time, 6.9 of every 1,000 women died in childbirth, and one in five children never made it beyond the age of five. By the year 2000 the number of children per family had fallen even further to 0.9.
>
> The average Total Fertility Rate (TFR) for the world, as of 2013, is 2.45. This shows the average number of children per woman alive, presuming she lived throughout the whole of her reproductive cycle. However, there is a wide variation between different country averages, from 0.79 in Singapore and 1.41 in Italy to figures as high as 2.55 in India and even 6.17 in Somalia.
>
> The average family size in the UK is 1.9, though the biggest family in Britain (at time of going to print) has 16 children.

Find out first (PAGE 84)

1a Students work in pairs and try and guess the answers.

b Either ask students to go online and check the answers, or if you are short of time, elicit their ideas then give the answers, feeding in the extra information from the Culture notes.

ANSWERS:
1 **a** 7, **b** 3.5, **c** 0.9
2 2.45
3 Italy and Somalia
4 16

2 Students could discuss this in groups or as a class. Ask if students know how these figures compare to their country/ies. If you have time, they could go online and find out.

View (PAGE 84)

See *Teaching tips: Using the video material in the classroom*, page 24.

3 With weaker classes, write the following topics on the board to give students ideas: *school, food, clothing, accommodation, transport*. Students discuss possible problems in groups. When they have finished, elicit ideas and write them on the board.

4a ▶ Give students a few minutes to read through the questions and check they understand what to listen for. Play part one of the DVD for students to identify the false statements.

b Students compare answers in pairs, then watch again if necessary and check. In feedback, elicit answers and refer back to the ideas you wrote on the board in exercise 3 to see if any of the students' ideas were mentioned.

ANSWERS:
1 c   2 a   3 a   4 b

5 ▶ Students discuss the question in pairs. Elicit some of their ideas. Play part two of the DVD for students to watch and check their answers. Choose a few students to report back and answer the question.

ANSWERS:
He thinks they are excellent and exceptional, and that people can learn a lot from them.

6 Students discuss the questions in groups.

World view (PAGE 85)

7a ▶ Go through the questions and check students understand what to listen for. Students watch the DVD and make notes.

b Students compare notes in pairs. Ask them to discuss what they can remember about the reasons the speakers give.

8 If necessary, play the DVD again for students to check. In feedback, ask a different student to summarise each speaker's answers.

ANSWERS:
Abigail: British; getting smaller; weaker – families are more disjointed and grandparents don't live with the family.

Sayful: Bangladeshi; getting smaller; stronger – siblings help each other financially, e.g. buying a house, investing in a business.

Luis: Spanish; smaller – less money; weaker – family members live apart, in different towns and countries.

Ciara: Irish; a bit smaller – mothers go out to work more than in the past; stronger – because people live apart, they always make an effort to come together on special occasions.

Paulona: Chinese; smaller – expensive housing and longer working hours; weaker – parents used to hand things down to their children, but because they now work longer hours, the children spend more time with maids and less with parents.

9 Students discuss the questions in groups.

Find out more ⊚ (PAGE 85)

10 Give students time to read through the questions and choose which topic they want to research online. Students can work alone or in groups, depending on how big your class is. Make sure students know they will be presenting their findings to the class, so they need to make notes in order to be able to do so. Monitor and help with vocabulary where necessary.

Find out more, exercise 10: Alternative suggestions

a If you have a multilingual class, you could ask students to choose three or four of the questions from all the topics and find the answers related to their country.

b If you have a monolingual class, you could ask students to choose a different country they'd like to find out about, and choose three or four of the questions from all the topics to research answers for.

Present your research

11 Go through the prompts, eliciting possible endings, and read the Tip with the class. Give students plenty of time to prepare their presentations, and help with vocabulary where necessary. When they are ready, students take turns presenting their findings. Encourage other students to listen and make notes, so that they can ask questions at the end of each presentation.

Students can now do Progress Test 4 on the Teacher's Resource Disc.

Grammar practice (PAGES 142–143)

See *Teaching tips: Using the Grammar and Vocabulary practice sections*, page 25.

Infinitives and *-ing* forms

ANSWERS:

1
1 possible for you to send
2 keen to make ('anxious' or 'determined' are also possible)
3 anxious about meeting
4 delighted to see
5 afraid of flying
6 advisable for you to take
7 wrong to be
8 determined not to let

2
1 All attempts to resolve the conflict peacefully have failed.
2 You will have the opportunity to meet the actors after the performance.
3 How will the government's plans to build 250,000 new homes affect property prices?
4 What do you think of the company's decision to hire a new manager from outside?
5 Did Kelly's refusal to sign the contract surprise you?
6 Does the thought of moving abroad next month worry you?
7 There was no need to be so rude to the waiter.
8 Did you have any difficulty finding a job after you graduated?

4
1 f disagree   2 i bother   3 a open   4 g tell   5 c stay
6 e tidy up   7 d be   8 h discuss   9 b slam   10 j go

5
1 congratulate her **on**   2 were prevented **from**   3 charged **with**
4 accusing you **of**   5 forgive Tony **for**   6 criticised **for**
7 blame you **for**   8 discourage my son **from**

6
1 to leave   2 help   3 having to   4 tapping
5 doesn't approve of   6 on you paying   7 face

8
1 The DJ kept us dancing all night, playing our favourite music.
2 The old man went off down the road, muttering to himself.
3 Taking a short cut through the back streets, we found a lovely little café.
4 Vanessa sat on the bus, thinking about what Mike had said.
5 Can you hear that strange noise coming from downstairs?
6 I heard the boy next door practising his trombone for hours.

9
1 appalled/horrified/concerned/shocked   2 plan(s)
3 explain   4 consider/justify   5 afford   6 sacrifice/ruin
7 makes   8 look/seem/appear   9 building   10 living
11 face   12 doing/trying

Vocabulary practice (PAGE 159)

Characteristics and behaviour

ANSWERS:

1
1 sulking   2 neat freak   3 hyperactive   4 messing around
5 overbearing   6 highly strung   7 irritable   8 laid-back
9 fussy   10 kept herself to herself

just

ANSWERS:

2a
1 just after the government had announced a
2 That's just the colour I wanted to
3 it was just awful
4 Could I just ask you to sit
5 and it's just 99 cents

2b
a 5   b 2   c 1   d 3   e 4

Other words and phrases

ANSWERS:

3
1 conscience-stricken   2 asking too much
3 make a snap decision   4 exchanged confidences
5 thick-skinned   6 had it all

09 THINGS TO COME

OVERVIEW

PAGES 86–87

Vocabulary and speaking: Describing future developments

Common European Framework: Students can scan quickly through long and complex texts, locating relevant details; can express their ideas and opinions with precision.

PAGES 88–89

Grammar review: Future forms

Listening and speaking: Living by numbers

Patterns to notice: Describing current trends

Common European Framework: Students can understand TV news and current affairs programmes; can use language flexibly and effectively.

PAGES 90–91

Reading and speaking: From fantasy to reality: How science fiction has influenced technology

Wordspot: *way*

Common European Framework: Students can understand specialised articles; can formulate ideas and opinions with precision.

PAGES 92–93

Task: Present a fantasy invention

Common European Framework: Students can give a clear, well-structured presentation of a complex subject, expanding and supporting points of view at some length with subsidiary points, reasons and relevant examples.

PAGES 94–95

Speaking: Explaining technical problems

Writing: Demanding urgent action

Common European Framework: Students can give clear, detailed descriptions of complex subjects; can express themselves with clarity and precision in correspondence.

Vocabulary and speaking

(PAGES 86–87)

Describing future developments

See *Teaching tips: Working with lexis*, page 21.

WARM UP

Write the following statements on the board:

1 *We will never make a 32-bit operating system.*
2 *A rocket will never be able to leave the Earth's atmosphere.*
3 *There is not the slightest indication that nuclear energy will ever be obtainable.*
4 *The cinema is little more than a fad. What audiences really want to see is flesh and blood on the stage.*
5 *It will be years – and not in my time – before a woman will lead the party or become prime minister.*

Explain that these are all predictions made in the past about the future. Students work in pairs and discuss who they think made them. Elicit their ideas then give the answers (*1 Bill Gates, 2 the New York Times, 3 Albert Einstein, 4 Charlie Chaplin, 5 Margaret Thatcher*). If you have time, students can go online to find more failed predictions (possible search terms: *failed predictions, predictions which didn't come true*), then share them with the class.

1a Write the topics on the board, and elicit one or two ideas from the class as examples, writing them next to the relevant topics on the board. Put students into groups to think of more ideas. When they are ready, ask one student from each group to come to the board to write their ideas next to the relevant topics.

b Elicit/Check: *poachers* (people who steal animals from private land for food) and *calorific foods* (foods with a lot of calories). Students read the article and check their predictions in groups. In feedback, go through the ideas on the board and tick off any that were mentioned.

2 Students check the meanings in pairs, using dictionaries / mobile phones if they need to. Go around and help where necessary. Check pronunciation of *revolutionise* /revəˈluːʃənaɪz/, *infrastructure* /ˈɪnfrəstrʌktʃə/ and *sustainability* /səsteɪnəˈbɪlɪti/.

3a–b Give students a few minutes to consider their opinions and the possible consequences, before putting them into pairs to discuss. When they have finished, nominate students to share their ideas and have a brief class discussion.

4 If necessary, look at the first two items as an example. Students work in pairs to discuss the other pairs of phrases. Check answers with the class.

ANSWERS:
3 D   4 S   5 S   6 D   7 S   8 D

5 Students complete the table alone then check in pairs, before checking answers with the whole class. Check the shifting stress in the last item, i.e. *sustain, sustainability, sustainable*.

ANSWERS:
2 booming   3 emergence   4 emerging   5 expand
6 expanding   7 potentially   8 revolution   9 revolutionary
10 sustain   11 sustainable

6 Read the example with the class. Students make predictions in groups. Go around and help with ideas and vocabulary, writing any new words/phrases on the board. When they have finished, ask a member of each group to read out their predictions and ask if other students agree.

Vocabulary and speaking, exercise 6: Alternative suggestion

Students go online to find out about predictions for the future (possible search terms: *future predictions, predictions for next 50 years, future timeline*). They then choose one to share with the class.

ADDITIONAL PRACTICE

Resource bank: Activity 9C *All change* (Describing future developments)

Vocabulary practice: Exercise 1

Workbook: Vocabulary: *Describing future developments*, page 44

76

Grammar review (PAGE 88)

Future forms

See *Teaching tips: Using a discovery approach to grammar*, page 20.

1   With weaker classes, you could ask them to read the Language summary on pages 144–145 and do exercises 1–3 in the Grammar practice on page 146 first. Alternatively, if you want to provide more challenge for your students, ask them to cover the list of forms at the top, then underline all the future forms they can find in the examples, and explain their use. They can then refer back to the list to see if they have found all the examples.

ANSWERS:

1 a   2 e, f   3 c   4 h   5 c   6 b   7 f, i   8 g   9 d   10 a

2   Students work through the questions in pairs. As they are working, go around and pay attention to any questions they are having difficulty with in order to focus on these more when you go through the answers.

ANSWERS:

1 *going to* (in sentence 6) is making a prediction based on evidence currently available.
2 The phrase *as soon as* is similar in function to *if*. This is actually similar to a first conditional sentence. In first conditional sentences, the present simple is used in the main (*if*) clause, and *will* is used in the other clause.
3 It is describing what people think *will happen* in the future, but from a point in the past. Therefore, *will* changes to *would*.
4 The sentence imagines a point (50 years) in the future, and looks back in time from that point.
5 Sentence 8: we use the Future continuous for things which will occur regularly and as part of the normal course of events in the future.
6 There is no future form of *can*. We need to use *will + be able to*.

Notes on future forms

Students often find future forms difficult in English, simply because there are so many of them. Another thing that makes them difficult to understand and use correctly is that it doesn't always depend on how we see the future event, but also how we *want* it to be seen. For example, if you know your boss is looking for someone to do a difficult job at work, and they ask you what you are doing later that day, it would be better to reply *I'm working on another project.* rather than *I'm going to work on another project.*, as arrangements are harder to change than intentions.

It's important that students don't get too caught up in whether they are using the correct form for the correct situation, and better to focus on examples where the form used sounds wrong, e.g. *What will you do over the weekend?* instead of *What are you going to do over the weekend?*

You may want to ask students to read Language summary 9 on pages 144–145 for a more detailed explanation of future forms.

3   Students discuss in groups, before reporting back to the class.

ADDITIONAL PRACTICE

➡ **Resource bank:** Activity 9A *Future most likely* (Future forms)

Grammar practice: Exercise 1–8

Workbook: Grammar: *Future forms*, pages 44–45

Listening and speaking (PAGES 88–89)

Living by numbers

1   Go through the things in the box and tell students which you keep track of to demonstrate. Ask them to leave blank any that they don't track and don't want to.

2   Students compare their answers to exercise 1 in pairs and discuss the questions.

3a   🎧 9.1 Elicit/Check: *gut instinct* (something which you feel is right but don't know why) and *become mainstream* (become popular and well-known). Students listen and tick the things in exercise 1 that they hear. Check answers with the class.

ANSWERS:

time spent online, coffee consumed, weight, how much sleep you get, thoughts and feelings

b   Students answer the questions in pairs. If necessary, play the recording again for them to check.

ANSWERS:

1 gut instinct or memory
2 modern technology
3 a special fork (to track how many bites he's taken) and a tiny camera (to take photos every 30 seconds)
4 50 different aspects of her life, including caffeine intake, sleep patterns, time spent on social media, as well as thoughts and ideas.

4a   🎧 9.2 Students listen and make notes. Explain that you'll ask them to summarise what each person says afterwards.

b   Students compare answers in pairs, listening again if necessary. When they are ready, ask students to summarise each speakers' views for the class.

ANSWERS:

Charlotte: you learn nothing useful and waste time and money; she doesn't believe everything can be reduced to numbers; a typical male obsession; you can't measure important things like how sunshine makes you feel; spending more time with friends and family makes you a better person

Roger: thinks you can learn a lot of useful information about yourself related to health and being efficient; self-tracking helps you live better; he's used it to organise his time better; self-tracking can be sociable

---

Listening and speaking, exercise 4: Alternative suggestion

Put students into pairs, and ask each student to focus on just one of the speakers and make notes. When they are ready, students summarise their speaker's points for their partner. They then listen again and check their partner's summary.

PATTERNS TO NOTICE

Describing current trends

1–3 To get students thinking about the patterns before they look at the examples in the box, you could write the following sentences on the board and ask students where a verb, adverb or phrase could be added in the sentence:

- to convey the idea of change or development:

  Self-tracking is mainstream.
  (becoming)
  While most of us are drowning in a sea of data ...
  (increasingly feeling like we're)

- to add emphasis to the trend:

  Modern technology is making it easier for them to collect data.
  (and easier)
  More people are doing it.
  (and more)

Then ask students for more examples of verbs and adverbs used to describe trends and direct them to the box to check.

5 Students discuss the questions in groups. In feedback, nominate a student from each group to share their ideas with the class.

6 Set up the activity by asking students which areas the three example sentences are related to (i.e. education, the media and technology), and which are true or false in their country/ies. You could also remind students of the similarities between some of the patterns by getting them to suggest how the examples could be slightly rewritten without changing the meaning, e.g.

Public exams are getting more and more difficult.
The quality of TV programmes is rapidly getting worse.
Computers are quickly becoming more sophisticated.

Students then work individually on their own true and false sentences using the trends listed.

7 Put students into small groups to read out their sentences and try to guess the false ones.

ADDITIONAL PRACTICE

➡ **Resource bank:** Activity 9B *Times are changing* (Describing current trends)

Workbook: Grammar: *Describing current trends*, page 46

Reading and speaking (PAGES 90–91)

From fantasy to reality: How science fiction has influenced technology

WARM UP

Bring downloaded posters or pictures of some major science fiction films and show them to students. Students discuss which they've seen and which they liked / didn't like in pairs.

1 Introduce the topic by giving one or two examples (e.g. *1984* predicting that we would all be watched by CCTV). Students discuss the questions in groups. In feedback, elicit students' ideas and write them on the board.

2 Focus attention on the title and elicit some predictions. You could also ask students to think of predictions made in the past which didn't come true. Students read the article and check their ideas.

3 Students read the article again and check the statements then check in pairs. In feedback, check answers with the class and elicit the part of the text that gives the answer.

ANSWERS:

1 F (The writer says 'Instead of ...'.)
2 T (He says that 'making predictions is tricky' and talks about 'disappointments'.)
3 F (He says that they are 'clunky' and it isn't always good to see the bored expression on someone else's face.)
4 T (He says that 'we quickly forget the astonishment of invention'.)
5 T (We are not 'disease-free' despite what fiction predicted.)
6 T (He says it is 'astonishing'.)
7 F (Only the first two things have come true.)

> **Reading, exercise 3: Alternative suggestion**
>
> To add an element of competition, do this activity as a race. The first pair to find all the answers wins.

4 Students work in pairs then check answers with the whole class. Check pronunciation of *inception* /ɪnˈsepʃən/ and *amputee* /ˌæmpjuˈtiː/.

ANSWERS:

inception = the time it was first thought of
clunky = not smooth
utter = complete, total
outstrips = does better than
pinprick-sized = tiny – as small as the end of a pin
amputees = people who have lost an arm or leg
non-invasive = surgery that doesn't involve cutting the body open

5 Students discuss the statements in groups, giving reasons for their opinions. When they have finished, ask a few students to report back to the class and have a brief class discussion.

ADDITIONAL PRACTICE

➡ **Workbook:** Listen and read: *5 ways parents can use technology*, pages 46–47

Wordspot (PAGE 91)

way

See *Teaching tips: Working with lexis*, page 21.

1a You could start by seeing which phrases with *way* students already know, e.g. *by the way, the best way of doing something*.

ANSWERS:

1 the way forward   **2** No way   **3** ask the way
4 have their own way   **5** on the way   **6** way too big for you

b Students complete the word web alone then check in pairs before checking answers with the whole class.

ANSWERS:

1 find the way   **2** know the way   **3** on the way
4 out of the way   **5** the wrong way up   **6** pave the way
7 underway   **8** way too   **9** go out of their way

2a Students can work in pairs to complete the conversations.

b 🎧 **9.3** Play the recording for students to check their answers. Students could practise the conversations in pairs.

ANSWERS:

1 in the way   **2** ask the way   **3** No way, way too old
4 went out of their way   **5** know the way, lead the way
6 underway   **7** on the way   **8** the wrong way round

ADDITIONAL PRACTICE
➡ **Resource bank:** Activity 9D *Where there's a will, there's a way* (*way*)
Vocabulary practice: Exercise 2
Workbook: Wordspot: *way*, page 47

Task (PAGES 92–93)
Present a fantasy invention
See *Teaching tips: Making tasks work*, page 23.

WARM UP
Ask students to go online and search online gadget shops or crowdsourcing websites to find interesting inventions, which they then share with the class.

Preparation (PAGES 92–93)
Listening and speaking

1a Check understanding of *technically viable* (actually possible). Students read the description of the programme. Check the class understands how it works.

> **ANSWER:**
> Contestants need to persuade a studio audience about which invention would be most practical or entertaining.

b Look at the first one or two entries with the class as examples. Students discuss the entries in pairs before sharing their ideas with the class.

2 🎧 9.4 Elicit/Check: *mislay* (lose temporarily), *swings and slides* (playground objects which you sit on and swing backwards and forwards (swings) and slide down (slides)), *trampolines* (something you jump up and down on) and *sat navs* (satellite navigations system that you use in your car). Students listen and make notes, then answer the questions in pairs before checking answers with the whole class.

> **ANSWERS:**
> **Speaker 1:** an AnythingFinder: it would be a small device which you could attach to everyday objects, which you could link to your phone
> **Speaker 2:** an adult-use playground: it would be a play area for adults, instead of going to the gym
> **Speaker 3:** a BusStopper: it would be a bus pass which allows you to communicate with the driver, to avoid missing your bus
> **Speaker 4:** a measurement photo app: an app on your phone that measured everything you took photos of
> **Speaker 5:** a TailgateLoser: a sign at the back of your car that communicates to cars which are too close behind

3 Answer the question as a class, playing the recording again if necessary.

> **ANSWERS:**
> **Speaker 1:** For people who often mislay everyday objects.
> **Speaker 2:** For adults, of all ages, who don't like going to the gym.
> **Speaker 3:** For bus passengers who often miss their bus in the morning.
> **Speaker 4:** For shoppers who want to buy the right furniture, or clothes.
> **Speaker 5:** For safe drivers who want to stick to the speed limit.

4 Focus attention on the phrases in the Useful language box. Students listen again and tick the phrases they hear.

> **ANSWERS:**
> **Speaker 1:** It would be (a small device) that …, It would save stress and time.
> **Speaker 2:** (This idea) makes perfect sense., It would be a great way of (socialising).
> **Speaker 3:** There would be a chip/camera built in that would …, How many times have you (wished you could …)?
> **Speaker 4:** I think there could be a real market for it.
> **Speaker 5:** My invention would be very (simple).

5 Students discuss the questions in pairs.

Task (PAGES 92–93)
Speaking

1a Give students plenty of time for this. Go around and help with vocabulary, writing any new words/phrases on the board.

b Students compare ideas in groups. You could ask them to choose the three or four best ideas.

2a–b With larger classes, put students into pairs. With smaller classes, they can work alone. Remind students of the phrases in the Useful language box, sections a and b and to use the checklist in order to structure their talks.

3 Students practise their presentations in pairs. While they are doing this, monitor and help where necessary, encouraging students to be persuasive.

4a–b Students present their ideas to the class. Encourage the 'audience' to ask follow-up questions and to challenge the ideas. Hold a class vote for the best invention at the end.

Follow up (PAGE 93)
Writing

1 Encourage students to use their notes from exercise 2b and the phrases from the Useful language box. When they have finished, students swap articles with another student to read.

> **Share your task**
> Some additional ideas could include:
> • Students prepare slides using presentation software to show details of their invention. They film themselves using these slides when presenting their ideas.
> • Give students an amount of money to invest in different ideas that they watch/listen to, explaining their reasons.
> • Once all the presentations have been filmed/recorded, hold an 'awards ceremony' and give different awards to different inventions, e.g. *Most creative*, *Cheapest to make*, etc.

Language live (PAGES 94–95)

Speaking (PAGE 94)
Explaining technical problems

1 To introduce the topic, tell students about the last time you had a technical problem, and what you did. Students discuss the questions in pairs before sharing ideas with the class.

2a 🎧 9.5 Tell students not to worry too much about technical vocabulary at this stage, as they'll have a chance to look at that in more detail afterwards. Play the recording for them to identify the problem and check in pairs, before checking answers with the whole class.

> **ANSWERS:**
> 1 a laptop won't connect to the internet
> 2 a phone can't find a signal
> 3 the cash till won't open

b Students complete the sentences in pairs, then listen again and check. Check answers with the class. Check pronunciation of *router* /'ruːtə/, *jammed* /'dʒæmd/ and *temperamental* /ˌtemprə'mentəl/.

> **ANSWERS:**
> 1 internet   2 router   3 error   4 reboot   5 hard   6 hard
> 7 scroll   8 illegal   9 update   10 create   11 crashed
> 12 reset   13 jammed   14 blank   15 temperamental
> 16 press   17 trial   18 off, on

> **Speaking, exercise 2b: Alternative suggestion**
> With weaker classes, or if you think most of this vocabulary will be new for your students, write the answers on the board in random order before they do exercise 2b. Ask them to fill the gaps in the conversations with the words before listening and checking.

3 Students discuss the questions in pairs. When they have finished, ask a few students to report back to the class and find out if anyone has similar ideas.

4a Go through the examples with the class, then ask students to write more questions in pairs. Go around and help with vocabulary where necessary. When they are ready, elicit students' questions and write them on the board.

b Students practise the conversations in pairs, switching roles after the first time and practising again.

Writing (PAGES 94–95)
Demanding urgent action

1 You could start by telling the class about the last time you had to return something, and what the outcome was, before asking students to share their own experiences with the class.

2 Give students a few minutes to read the emails then discuss which is more effective in pairs.

> **ANSWERS:**
> **A** a tablet computer   **B** a printer
> Email B is more effective, because it is more organised, is less emotional, and gets to the point quickly.

3a Students answer the questions in pairs before checking answers with the whole class. As you go through the answers, elicit examples of each feature where possible.

> **ANSWERS:**
> 1 A   2 B   3 A   4 B   5 B   6 A   7 A   8 B   9 B   10 A

b Students put the things in order then check in pairs. Check answers with the class.

> **ANSWERS:**
> 2, 5, 3, 1, 4

4 When students have compared phrases in pairs, elicit ideas with the class and write them on the board.

5a Refer students to the information on page 108 and explain that they should choose the most appropriate information.

b Students organise the information, comparing with the order in exercise 3b, then write the first draft of their emails. Go around and help with vocabulary, writing any new words/phrases on the board.

6 Students swap drafts. Remind them of the key features in exercise 3a and encourage them to make suggestions. Students write their final drafts in class or for homework.

ADDITIONAL PRACTICE

➡ **Workbook:** Language live: *Explaining technical problems*, page 48; Writing: *Demanding urgent action*, page 48

Grammar practice (PAGES 146–147)

See *Teaching tips: Using the Grammar and Vocabulary practice sections*, page 25.

Future forms

> **ANSWERS:**
> 1
> 2 *will still be* is a prediction about now.
> 4 *won't start* means 'refuses to'.
> 7 *I'll often have* refers to a present habit.
> 9 *shall* here is used to ask for a suggestion.
> 2
> 1 *'m leaving* – it's 100% certain.
> 2 both are acceptable
> 3 *we see* – *will* is not possible in a clause after *whichever/wherever*, etc.
> 4 both are acceptable
> 5 both are acceptable as a prediction in this case, because it could be based on either present evidence, or the speaker's feelings/ expectations.
> 6 *Shall we get* – it's clear that this is a suggestion, not a question about an intention, because of the reply 'OK, good idea'.
> 7 *going to lose* – because it's an intention, not a definite arrangement.
> 8 *I'll buy* – it's a decision made at the moment of speaking.
> 3
> 1 will have been living   2 'll be   3 'll have been driving
> 4 will have gone   5 'll have chosen   6 'll never find
> 4a
> 1 be implanted   2 be allocated   3 be reading / read
> 4 be living / live   5 be working / work   6 be committed   7 own
> 5
> 1 Ryan Lewington is to sign (is going to sign) a £5 million contract to play for United.
> 2 A new manager is unlikely to be announced until after the summer.
> 3 We are due to meet the client at 9:00 a.m. tomorrow.
> 4 O'Reilly is set to receive a life sentence after today's guilty verdict.
> 5 The film's about to start – come on!
> 6 Brazil are bound to win the World Cup this year.

6

    1 e – is due to play (planned for a certain time)
    2 c – is set to announce (this is likely to happen)
    3 b – are to be provided (this has been officially arranged)
    4 a – is set to do (this is likely to happen)
    5 d – is to get (this has been officially arranged)
    6 f – is due to open (planned for a certain time)

7

    1 c (an intention in the past)
    2 f (a plan in the past)
    3 g (he became his boss later but Pete didn't anticipate this at the time)
    4 i (something planned which did not take place)
    5 h (an intention in the past)
    6 a (the decision changed his life, but he didn't anticipate this at the time)
    7 j (something planned which did not take place)
    8 e (a prediction in the past)
    9 b (he regretted his choice later, but he didn't anticipate this at the time)
    10 d (he regretted his impulse later, but he didn't anticipate this at the time)

Vocabulary practice (PAGE 160)

Describing future developments

ANSWERS:

1

    1 sustainable   **2** pave the way   **3** caught on   **4** met with
    5 become a reality   **6** massive boom   **7** fulfil her potential
    8 underway

way

ANSWERS:

2

    1 as **the** way forward
    2 Your essay is ~~too way~~ **way too** long
    3 I'm ~~in~~ **on** the way
    4 I don't know ~~a~~ **the** way
    5 you'll only get ~~on~~ **in** the way
    6 the wrong way ~~down~~ **up / round**
    7 ~~Not~~ **No** way will we
    8 Don't let her have ~~the~~ **her** own way

Other words and phrases

ANSWERS:

3

    1 are yet to   **2** non-invasive   **3** tricky   **4** pinpoint the cause
    5 it came to pass   **6** surpassed / outstripped

OVERVIEW

PAGES 96–97

Vocabulary and speaking: Truth and lies

Common European Framework: Students can use a broad range of language allowing them to select a formulation to express themselves clearly; can give clear, detailed descriptions.

PAGES 98–99

Listening: Living a lie

Patterns to notice: Phrases with *as … as* + verb

Wordspot: *well*

Common European Framework: Students can understand extended speech even when it is not clearly structured and when relationships are only implied and not signalled explicitly; can easily follow and contribute to complex interactions.

PAGES 100–101

Reading and speaking: How do you know if someone is lying?

Grammar review: Ellipsis and substitution

Common European Framework: Students can understand in detail lengthy, complex texts, whether or not they relate to their own area of speciality; can express themselves fluently and spontaneously.

PAGES 102–103

Task: Detect the lies

Common European Framework: Students can express their ideas and opinions with precision, present and respond to complex lines of argument convincingly.

PAGES 104–105

World culture: Cyber crime

Common European Framework: Students can understand a wide range of recorded and broadcast audio material; can give a clear, well-structured presentation of a complex subject.

Vocabulary and speaking

(PAGES 96–97)

Truth and lies

See *Teaching tips: Working with lexis*, page 21.

WARM UP

Tell the class some of the lies you've told in the last week. Students then make a list of some of the lies they've told then compare in pairs. In feedback, find out if any students had answers in common.

1 Focus attention on the pictures and elicit/check: *white lie* (small, unimportant lie that you tell to make someone feel better or avoid hurting their feelings). Students discuss the questions in groups, then share ideas with the class.

2 Give students a few minutes to read the situations and discuss their answers with a partner. You may want to check that students understand the vocabulary in bold in the text before they start reading.

POSSIBLE ANSWERS:

1 lying **2** telling the truth **3** not clear **4** lying **5** lying
6 lying **7** telling the truth **8** lying **9** lying **10** lying
11 lying **12** not clear **13** lying

3 Students work individually or in pairs, then check with the whole class. Check pronunciation of *exaggerating* /ɪɡˈzædʒəreɪtɪŋ/ (making something seem better or bigger than it is), *perjury* /ˈpɜːdʒəri/ (telling a lie in a court of law), *plagiarism* /ˈpleɪdʒərɪzm/ (using someone else's words or writing and pretending they're yours) and *hoax* /həʊks/ (making people believe something that isn't true, usually in the media, or a false warning about something dangerous).

POSSIBLE ANSWERS:

a 4 **b** 3 **c** 1 **d** 5 **e** 7 **f** 9 **g** 11 **h** 8 **i** 10 **j** 6
k 12 **l** 13 **m** 2

4a You could do an example with the class first, then give students time to reread the situations and choose their comments.

b Students compare answers in pairs. In feedback, ask one or two students to report back on any situations they disagreed about.

5 Students can work individually or help each other to add the vocabulary to the word web in pairs.

ANSWERS:

1 home truths
2 embellish the facts, pass something off, tell a white lie, make an excuse, exaggerate, tell tales, tell a fib
3 testify under oath, commit perjury, con people out of money, plagiarism, commit forgery, carry out a hoax, bogus /ˈbəʊɡəs/ (something which is not real or true, e.g. *a bogus $20 note*, *a bogus insurance claim*)
4 cheat on someone, spread malicious gossip (usually about people's personal lives), tell someone a rumour (also used in other contexts when something is talked about as 'news', although there is no proof that it is true. A common phrase is: *There's a rumour going around that …*)
5 illicit, under a false impression, tactful, deceive, do harm, immoral, trust, unscrupulous

get away with and *be taken in* could go in any of the categories apart from 'ways of telling the truth' – you could ask students to explain why (i.e. because they both imply that people believe the lie).

ADDITIONAL PRACTICE

Resource bank: Activity 10C *What did you say?* (Truth and lies)

Vocabulary practice: Exercises 1 & 2

Workbook: Vocabulary: *Truth and lies*, page 49

Listening (PAGES 98–99)

Living a lie

1   Introduce the topic by eliciting some of the situations an undercover police officer might work in (e.g. fighting the drugs trade, terrorism, etc.). Students discuss the questions in pairs.

2a Students categorise the words/phrases in pairs, then check ideas with the class.

b   🎧 10.1 Elicit/Check: *(police) baton* (stick police officers use to defend themselves), *battered and bruised* (injured, hurt) and *become estranged* (become separated). Students listen and mark the sentences alone then check in pairs. Check answers with the class.

ANSWERS:

1 F (He was a 'transport police officer'.)
2 F (He was an 'unconventional father' and 'was frequently away'.)
3 F (He was asked because 'he was good at his job'.)
4 F (It was because he 'always seemed to have as much money as he needed'.)
5 T

3a Students discuss the question in pairs then as a class.

b   🎧 10.2 Play the recording for students to check their answer to exercise 3a, then answer the questions in pairs. Check answers with the class.

POSSIBLE ANSWERS:

3a
Sentences 1 and 2 are correct.
b
1 Jon was attacked by a police officer.
2 He and his wife grew distant from each other.
3 His fellow activists.
4 The activists were planning to shut down an oil refinery.
5 Because he was arrested, even though the police knew his real identity.

4   Elicit students' predictions and write their ideas on the board for them to refer back to while listening.

5   🎧 10.3 Students listen and check their predictions in exercise 4, then answer the questions in pairs. Check answers with the class.

ANSWERS:

1 The police thought that he was too involved with the activists; the activists thought he was too involved with the police.
2 He was told his mission was ending, and there was no future work for him in the police force.
3 His girlfriend found his passport.
4 He was asked to defend six of the activists who wanted to close down the oil refinery.
5 Jon's ex-girlfriend, and Jon himself.

6   Students discuss the questions in groups.

PATTERNS TO NOTICE

Phrases with *as … as* + verb

1   Write the example sentences on the board and ask students to complete them. Establish that the pattern is used to emphasise how much money he had and how soon he had to get out.

ANSWERS:

1 as, needed   2 as, could

2   Focus students on the table and point out that quantifiers like *much* and *many* can also be used between *as … as*. Ask students for some examples of verbs for the first column, e.g.
   • have as many as you want
   • come as soon as you can
   • stay as long as you need
   • come and see us as often as you like

Demonstrate that the main stress falls on the adverb or quantifier by reading a few of the phrases aloud. Help students to say them naturally by starting with just the verbs and adverb/quantifier, e.g.
   • have → many → want
   • come → soon → can
   • stay → long → need
   • come → see → often → like

Then get them to say the phrases again with the same rhythm, with the other words 'squashed' in between:
   • have [as] many [as you] want
   • come [as] soon [as you] can
   • stay [as] long [as you] need
   • come [and] see [us as] often [as you] like

Potential problem with *as … as* + verb

A common mistake with this form is to use a comparative adjective, e.g. *My car is as faster as yours.* Make sure students understand that this pattern is used to emphasise rather than compare.

---

7   Students can work on the answers individually or in pairs.

POSSIBLE ANSWERS:

2 We can leave as soon as you want.
3 You can buy as many as you want.
4 Take me as far as you can.
5 Spend as long as you need.
6 No, eat as much as you can.
7 We went swimming as often as we could/wanted.
8 I'll get there as soon as I can.
9 You can invite as many as you want.
10 We're walking as fast as we can!
11 Keep them as long as you want/need.

Listening, exercise 7: Alternative suggestion

To give students a little more challenge, make this a speaking activity – students take turns to read a question at random from the list, for their partner to answer orally as quickly as possible.

ADDITIONAL PRACTICE

➡ **Resource bank:** Activity 10B *Say the phrases* (Phrases with *as … as* + verb)

Workbook: Grammar: *Phrases with* as … as + *verb*, page 50

Wordspot (PAGE 99)

well

See *Teaching tips: Working with lexis*, page 21.

1   You could start by putting the following gapped phrases on the board, and asking students what the missing word common to all of them is.
'I passed my exams.' '... done!'
'I'm not feeling very ... .'
'Did you sleep ... ?'
'It may ... rain tomorrow.'
Then get them to explain why *well* is used in each case. Focus students on the word web and give them a few minutes to underline any new uses/examples of *well*.

> **Wordspot, exercise 1: Alternative suggestion**
> If you want to give students more challenge, copy the word web, removing the underlined definitions. Students have to look at the examples for each use of *well* and write their own definition. Then they can look at the word web in the book to check.

2   You may want to read out examples 1–8 for students to hear how the interjection is said in each case. They can mark the meanings in the box with the appropriate number as you read each one. You could then read out the examples again for students to copy the intonation.

ANSWERS:
1 to show surprise   2 for emphasis   3 to show anger/annoyance
4 to express doubt   5 to pause   6 to continue a story
7 to accept a situation   8 to show you've finished

3a Put students into pairs to discuss the adjectives and to check any they're not sure of in a dictionary or on their mobile phones. Then point out to the class that the stress always falls on the participle, not on *well*, and that in the cases where the participle contains a particle (*well-laid-out*, *well-looked-after*, *well-thought-out*), the stress falls on the particle. Check that students understand the following: *well-built* is used to talk about people, not buildings; *well-earned* is used to talk about something you deserve, not money – a common collocation is 'a well-earned rest'; *well-read* is used to describe people who have read a lot.

b   Put students into pairs or small groups to discuss the things/people in the box.

POSSIBLE ANSWERS:
books: well-written, well-informed, well-laid-out, well-prepared, well-thought-out
children: well-behaved, well-dressed, well-educated, well-fed, well-looked-after
shops: well-laid-out
exam candidates: well-behaved, well-educated, well-informed, well-prepared, well-read
teacher: well-behaved, well-educated, well-informed, well-paid, well-prepared, well-read
a holiday: well-chosen, well-earned, well-prepared
babies: well-fed, well-looked-after
a potential husband/wife: well-balanced, well-behaved, well-chosen
everyone: well-balanced, well-behaved, well-educated, well-informed, well-fed, well-looked-after, well-paid, well-read

4   Read out the first example to the class, showing how *well* is stressed. Put students into pairs to do the rest of the examples and to practise reading the sentences with the stress on *well*.

ANSWERS:
2 By the time we got home, it was **well** after eight o'clock.
3 Personally, I think the end results have been **well** worth the effort.
4 As you **well** know / know **well**, you are not allowed to smoke in here.
5 By the time they arrived – **well** over two hours late – I was truly fed up.
6 Marta is **well** ahead of the other students in the class.
7 The Chinese were using paper money **well** before people in the West.

> **Wordspot, exercise 4: Alternative suggestion**
> Put students into teams, and ask them to do the exercise orally. Make sure they don't write any answers at this stage. After a few minutes, do a board race. Each turn, call out one of the numbers 2–7 at random, and someone from each team must come to the board and write the sentence with *well* in the correct place (if you have an IWB, students could write the sentence on a piece of paper which they hold up when finished). The first team to do so gets a point, and the team with the most points at the end wins. Afterwards, ask students to do the exercise on their own and check answers.

ADDITIONAL PRACTICE

➡ **Resource bank:** Activity 10D *Well done!* (*well*)
Vocabulary practice: Exercise 3
Workbook: Wordspot: *well*, page 50

Reading and speaking (PAGES 100–101)

How do you know if someone is lying?

WARM UP

Put students into teams. Each turn, read out one of the lies below (you may wish to refer students back to the vocabulary on pages 96–97 of the Students' Book first). The first team to say which kind of lie it is gets a point, and the team with the most points wins.
1 I love your new haircut, it's definitely not too short.
2 No, I didn't eat the last biscuit.
3 I'm sorry, but I've been seeing someone else.
4 Sorry I'm late, the traffic was a nightmare.
5 There must have been hundreds and hundreds of people in the shop.
6 Have you heard about Judy? Apparently she lied about her experience in the interview.
7 It's about time you pulled yourself together and went out and started meeting people.
(Answers: 1 telling a white lie, 2 telling a fib, 3 cheating on someone, 4 making an excuse, 5 exaggerating, 6 spreading malicious gossip, 7 telling a few home truths)

1   Either discuss these questions with the whole class or put students into small groups to discuss them.

2a Put students into pairs to do this, then collect their ideas on the board.

b   While students are reading, they could underline any ways which they listed, and circle any ways which they did not think of.

ANSWERS:
The article lists the following ways: dry mouth, higher blood pressure, faster breathing, increased flow of electricity to the skin, voice changes, hesitation, blushing.

3 Give students time to reread the text, then put them into pairs to discuss their answers.

ANSWERS:
1 **b** is true – the stress, not the rice, makes your mouth go dry.
2 **a** is true – if it is done involuntarily or 'under duress', the extra stress makes it unreliable; **b** is also true – they rely on changes in blood pressure, breathing rate, and the amount we sweat.
3 **a** is true; **b** is not true because it measures stress patterns in your voice, not how stressed you are; **c** – is not true because it is cheap but not reliable.
4 All three answers are true.
5 **a** and **b** are true; **c** is not true because the text says it 'could' be used, not that it is already in use.

4 Give students time to find the words in the text, then discuss possible alternatives in pairs.

ANSWERS:
examination – *test*
hand – *give* ('hand' is often used as a regular verb)
bodily – *physical*
under duress – *by force*
premise – *assumption*
other half – *partner, husband or wife* (very informal)
picking up – *detecting*
mentally considering – *deciding, thinking about*
getting – *being*
high-profile – *attracting public attention*

5 Put students into small groups to discuss the questions, then ask one or two groups to report back on the most interesting points from their discussion.

> **Reading and speaking, exercise 5: Alternative suggestion**
> Make the discussion into a 'ranking' activity. Give students criteria such as 'reliability', 'appeal' and 'cost', and ask them to rank the five techniques from 1–5 under each of the criteria. They could do this individually, then compare with a partner and justify their decisions.

ADDITIONAL PRACTICE
Workbook: Listen and read: *Believe it or not*, page 51

Grammar review (PAGE 101)
Ellipsis and substitution
See *Teaching tips: Using a discovery approach to grammar*, page 20.

1a Ask students to read the conversation quickly to see which method of lie detection the people are talking about. Then do the first example with the class and give students time to do the rest individually or in pairs.

b 🎧 **10.4** Play the recording for students to listen and check. Establish that the shortened forms are used to avoid repetition and make the sentence less 'clumsy'. As you go through the answers, check that students understand what changes have been made to the original sentence. It might be helpful to write the dialogue on the board or show it on a screen.

ANSWERS:
1 Oh yes, that ~~article about lie detectors~~ **one**.
2 ... but I didn't finish *reading* it.
3 Do they realise they are *blushing*?
4 I don't think ~~they realise they are blushing~~ **so**.
5 I don't ~~ever blush when I talk to you~~.
6 Of course it **is** *true*.
7 ~~I never lie to you, and you never lie to me~~ **We never lie to each other**, ...

2 Discuss this question with the whole class.

ANSWERS:
you = people in general. *We* can also be used here.
they = the other person. *He* or *She* could be used here if we know exactly who the person is.

You may want to ask students to read Language summary 10 on pages 148–149 for a more detailed explanation of ellipsis and substitution.

ADDITIONAL PRACTICE
Resource bank: Activity 10A *Urban legends* (Ellipsis and substitution)
Grammar practice: Exercises 1–8
Workbook: Grammar: *Ellipsis and substitution*, pages 51–53; Pronunciation: *Pronouns*, page 53

Task (PAGES 102–103)
Detect the lies
See *Teaching tips: Making tasks work*, page 23.

Preparation (PAGES 102–103)
Listening
1 Students read the rules then explain how the game works in pairs. Check understanding by asking students to summarise to the class.
2 🎧 **10.5** Students listen and answer the questions in pairs, then check answers with the whole class.

ANSWERS:
Player A
1 Skills and abilities you have
2 She says she is a nail technician, she can do manicures and pedicures; she is good at making cakes; she can type quickly; she makes her own jewellery; she's good at accountancy and book-keeping; she can train dogs.
3 She can't train dogs, make jewellery or bake cakes.
Player B
1 How you spent last weekend
2 He went to Newcastle; stayed in the honeymoon suite of a hotel; went to a music festival; had ice cream; had a huge meal; was delayed four hours on a train.
3 He didn't go to a music festival, stay in a honeymoon suite or have ice cream.

Task (PAGES 102–103)
Speaking

1 Give students plenty of time to prepare what they're going to say. Go through the Useful language box, section a with the class. Go around and help with ideas and vocabulary, writing any new words/phrases on the board.

2 Refer students back to the Useful language box. They then play the game in groups. Go around and help where necessary. When they have finished, ask students to share some of the lies they told and find out who got the most points in each group.

Share your task

Some additional ideas could include:

- Allocate different topics to different students, to ensure they film/record a range of topics.
- Students watch/listen to the recordings, and decide if the student is lying or telling the truth.
- Students film/record themselves telling a mix of lies and facts. Other students watch/listen and guess which is which.

World culture (PAGES 104–105)
Cyber crime

Culture notes

Insurance fraud is when someone makes a false insurance claim, i.e. they attempt to obtain a benefit which they are knowingly not entitled to obtain.

Types of insurance fraud can range from giving a slightly higher value of lost or stolen items to deliberately causing accidents or committing crimes in order to claim money.

Estimates of how much insurance fraud there actually is in the world are difficult to make, though organisations such as the Coalition Against Insurance Fraud in the USA estimates that in 2006 the figure was around $80 billion, while the Insurance Fraud Bureau estimates it to cost UK insurance firms around £1.5 billion a year.

Most insurance companies employ claims adjusters in order to investigate fraudulent claims, and this generally involves two steps: first, identifying suspicious claims compared to national averages, and secondly, special investigators carrying out detailed research into the cause of the claims to try and find out if fraudulent claims have taken place.

Find out first (PAGE 104)

1a Introduce the topic by asking what kinds of things people usually insure in the students' country/ies. Elicit/Check: *for scrap* (for the price of the metal it's made from). Students read the situations then discuss in pairs. Elicit any other situations they can think of. Encourage them to think back over any cases of fraud they've heard about in the news recently.

b Students discuss the question in pairs then as a class.

POSSIBLE ANSWER:

Because it costs them a lot of money, which means they then have to charge the customer more.

2a–b Students discuss in pairs, then either go online to check or check with you if short of time. Feed in the extra information from the Culture notes as you check answers.

POSSIBLE ANSWER:

Insurance companies employ claims adjustors, who compare suspicious claims to national averages and carry out detailed investigations into the claims.

View (PAGE 104)

See *Teaching tips: Using the video material in the classroom*, page 24.

3 ▶ Go through the questions and check students understand what to listen for. Play the DVD for students to answer the questions then check in pairs. Check answers with the class.

ANSWERS:

1 Symbols flash up on the screen which tell the operator how to continue.
2 He's an insurance investigator. Previously he worked for the Greater Manchester Police Force.
3 He stops the claim.

---

4 Students watch again and answer the questions, then check in pairs. Check answers with the class.

ANSWERS:

1 HR = High risk, SNS = Subject Not Sure
2 gut feeling and instinct
3 a watch
4 He asks him for specific details, e.g. the colour of the letters on the watch face.

---

5 Students discuss in pairs or as a class. Ask students how they'd feel about having the technology used on them.

World view (PAGE 105)

6a ▶ Give students time to read the sentences and check they know what to listen for. Play the DVD for students to watch and do the exercise.

b Students check in pairs, and discuss what other points and examples they heard. Play the DVD again for students to check. Nominate students to summarise what each speaker said to the class.

ANSWERS:

Heather: 2; Technology is advancing quickly and crime is becoming more technological, which makes it difficult for law enforcement to keep up.

Keith: 3; Crime isn't easier, but there are more new types of crimes, such as ID fraud, stealing bank details and personal information. At the same time, criminals leave a trace so should be easier to follow.

Imogen: 5; More CCTV makes more traditional crimes such as burglary more difficult.

Eben: 4; He heard someone say the internet is 'an experiment in chaos', i.e. we've never done it before. He says we are all like bits of code in a huge program.

Jurgen: 7; He has a games console which tracks him to find other players. If a burglar hacked into it, the burglar would be able to know when he wasn't at home.

Ciara: 1; Different criminal networks, e.g. gangs can get together and share information.

Keith: 8; It's a difficult area – to be more secure, we might need to give up some of our liberties. He says there are a lot of troubling issues around that.

Eben: 6; For criminals too it's probably also an experiment, but they are also bits of code so the question is how they can conceal themselves.

---

7 Students discuss the questions in groups, then as a class.

Find out more 🔊 (PAGE 105)

8 If you want to ensure students cover a range of the methods, you could allocate them to different students. Otherwise, let students choose which they want to research and go online. Monitor and help with vocabulary where necessary.

Present your research

9 Go through the prompts, eliciting possible endings, and read the Tip with the class. Give students plenty of time to prepare their presentations, and help with vocabulary where necessary. When they are ready, students take turns presenting their findings. Encourage other students to listen and make notes so that they can ask questions at the end of each presentation.

Students can now do Progress Test 5 and the End of course test on the Teacher's Resource Disc.

Grammar practice (PAGES 150–151)

See *Teaching tips: Using the Grammar and Vocabulary practice sections*, page 25.

Ellipsis and substitution

ANSWERS:

1
1 f – I already have ~~tidied my room~~.
2 c – No, we only ordered one ~~bottle of water~~.
3 b – Yeah, ~~it's a~~ good thing I brought an umbrella.
4 h – Yeah, ~~it's a~~ pity she couldn't stay longer.
5 a – No, I'm just going to ~~send Judy the templates~~.
6 d – ~~I have~~ no idea, ~~I'm~~ sorry.
7 e – ~~I'm~~ sorry, I don't drive.
8 g – I didn't ~~leave the back door open~~, it was Shelly.

2
1 They watched the street performers dancing energetically at the traffic lights.
2 The woman found guilty of the murder was sentenced to life imprisonment.
3 Of all the films directed by Shane Meadows, this is my favourite.
4 Despite jumping off the moving train, the stunt man was uninjured.
5 All new members receive a welcome pack containing a badge and a handbook.
6 Do you see that woman wearing the black dress? That's Paula.
7 Small dogs don't need so much space to run around in.
8 The information sent out in the email was wrong.
9 I've never heard of the woman giving the talk today.

3
1 I know he **does** – I met him in the lift the other day.
2 Well, if you **do**, could you buy milk?
3 I thought **so** – his face looked familiar.
4 **Nor did I.** Nobody told me he only speaks Russian.
5 Really? **So did we!** Where were you sitting?
6 I didn't expect them to provide me with lunch, but they **did**.
7 I think the blue **ones** would look better with those jeans.
8 No, it was the **one** with the diamonds.
9 I hope **so**, too.

5
1 You need to stick up for yourself more.
2 They just looked at each other.
3 We're trying to be nice to each other.
4 We don't love each other any more.
5 I prefer the black ones myself.
6 Did you really do it by yourself?
7 She blames herself for what happened.
8 Come on, pull yourself together.

6
1 that 2 that, This 3 this 4 this 5 this 6 that

7
1 if you don't **want to**.
2 ~~It~~ **They** said it's important.
3 ~~So don't~~ **Neither do I**!
4 it was ~~she~~ **her**!
5 seen ~~him~~ **them** perform live
6 Would you like to try ~~ones~~ **some**?
7 to ~~each another~~ **each other / one another**
8 'I think ~~do~~ **so**.'
9 all by ~~himself~~ **yourself**?
10 Nice **to** meet you.

8
2 Candi Prambanan 3 the theories 4 Princess Rara Jonggrang
5 Princess Rara Jonggrang 6 Prince Bandung
7 Prince Bandung and the spirits 8 the spirits 9 the princess
10 the statues

Vocabulary practice (PAGE 161)
Truth and lies

ANSWERS:

1
1 got away with it 2 home truths 3 plagiarism
4 spreading malicious gossip 5 cheating on him 6 exaggerating

2
1 committing forgery, plagiarism
2 committing perjury, testifying under oath
3 embellishing the facts, exaggerating
4 telling a fib, telling tales
5 telling a few home truths, telling a white lie

well

ANSWERS:

3
1 d – **Well**, you could have called.
2 a – I really don't feel **well**.
3 f – **Well** said!
4 b – It went **well**, fortunately
5 c – As **well** as being clever
6 e – it was **well** after midnight

Other words and phrases

ANSWERS:

4
1 providing us with accurate intelligence 2 dropped the charges
3 activists 4 reconcile 5 infiltrate 6 had my conviction

Pearson Education Limited
Edinburgh Gate
Harlow
Essex CM20 2JE
England
and Associated Companies throughout the world.

www.pearsonelt.com

First published 2014

ISBN: 978-1-4479-3682-4

Set in Bliss Light 8.5pt/10.5pt
Printed in Slovakia by Neografia

Cover images: *Front:* **SuperStock:** Radius

Illustrated by: Julian Mosedale

The publisher would like to thank the following for their kind
permission to reproduce their photographs:

(Key: b-bottom; c-centre; l-left; r-right; t-top)

Fotolia.com: javier brosch 7C (D), Elenathewise 1D (D residential
area), Ingus Evertovskis 1D (B demolition of old building), Faraways
1D (C overcrowding), foto6004 1D (A infrastructure), Alexandra Gl
1D (D congestion), hifashion 7C (B), MasterLu 1D (A reclaimed land),
Spectral-Design 1D (C high-rise buildings), trekandphoto 7C (A),
victoria p 1D (B green-belt land); Shutterstock.com: biletskiy 7C (E),
Ysbrand Cosijn 7Atl, Gabrielle Ewart 7Atr, Racheal Grazias 7Abr,
han871111 7C (C), InnervisionArt 7C (F), koya979 7Abl, Maridav 7C
(H), Catalin Petolea 7C (G)

All other images © Pearson Education Limited

Every effort has been made to trace the copyright holders and we
apologise in advance for any unintentional omissions. We would be
pleased to insert the appropriate acknowledgement in any subsequent
edition of this publication.